Avalanche of Grace!

Growing in Christian Virtues

(A Fifty-Day Devotional)

2 Corinthians 3: 16-18
[W]henever a person turns to the Lord, the veil is removed. Now the Lord is the Spirit, and where the Spirit of the Lord is, there is freedom. All of us, gazing with unveiled face on the glory of the Lord, are being transformed into the same image from glory to glory, as from the Lord who is the Spirit (New American Bible).

by
Dr. Annet Judith O'Mara

Xulon Press
2301 Lucien Way #415
Maitland, FL 32751
407.339.4217
www.xulonpress.com

© 2020 by Dr. Annet Judith O'Mara

All rights reserved solely by the author. The author guarantees all contents are original and do not infringe upon the legal rights of any other person or work. No part of this book may be reproduced in any form without the permission of the author. The views expressed in this book are not necessarily those of the publisher.

Unless otherwise indicated, Scripture texts in this work are taken from the New American Bible with Revised New Testament and Revised Psalms © 1991, 1986, 1970 Confraternity of Christian Doctrine, Washington, D.C. and are used by permission of the copyright owner. All Rights Reserved. No part of the New American Bible may be reproduced in any form without permission in writing from the copyright owner.

Printed in the United States of America.
ISBN-13: 978-1-6312-9675-8
Library of Congress Control Number: 2020911366

Contents

I. Dedication viii

II. Acknowledgments ix

III. Introduction. xi

IV. Disclaimers. xiii

V.   Avalanche of Grace!

Part One
Holy Trinity, Mold Me in Your Theological Virtues

1. Virtue of Faith 1

2. Virtue of Hope. 5

3. Virtue of Charity 11

Part Two
Holy Trinity, Mold Me in Your Cardinal Virtues

4. Virtue of Prudence 17

5. Virtue of Justice. .21

6.   Virtue of Fortitude 25

7.   Virtue of Temperance 29

Part Three
Holy Trinity, Mold Me in Your Beatitudal Virtues

8.   Virtue of Poverty 33

9.   Virtue of Mourning 37

10. Virtue of Meekness 41

11. Virtue of Righteousness 46

12. Virtue of Mercy 51

13. Virtue of Cleanliness of Heart 56

14. Virtue of Peace-Making 61

15. Virtue of Resilience 68

Part Four
Holy Trinity, Mold Me in Your Moral Virtues

16. Virtue of Contrition 73

17. Virtue of Repentance 80

18. Virtue of Reparation 85

19. Virtue of Balanced Passions. 89

20. Virtue of a Moral Conscience 94

Part Five
Holy Trinity, Mold Me in Your Sacrificial Virtues

21. Virtue of Detachment 102

22. Virtue of Total Abandonment 107

23. Virtue of Sacrifice 111

24. Virtue of Holy Indifference 116

Part Six
Holy Trinity, Mold Me in Your Social Justice Virtues

25. Virtue of Solidarity 122

26. Virtue of Kindness and Goodness 127

27. Virtue of Respect for Life 133

28. Virtue of Industry and Diligence 140

29. Virtue of Hospitality 146

30. Virtue of Magnanimity 155

Part Seven
Holy Trinity, Mold Me in Your Teleological Virtues

31. Virtue of Orderliness 163

32. Virtue of Discernment 171

33. Virtue of Patience 178

34. Virtue of Honor and Integrity 184

35. Virtue of Faithfulness 189

36. Virtue of Accountability 196

Part Eight
Holy Trinity, Mold Me in Your True Beauty Virtues

37. Virtue of Docility 201

38. Virtue of Simplicity 206

39. Virtue of Humility 212

40. Virtue of Trust 217

41. Virtue of Forgetting the Past 222

42. Virtue of True Beauty 227

Part Nine
Holy Trinity, Mold Me in Your Beatific Vision Virtues

43. Virtue of Holiness 233

44. Virtue of Joy 237

45. Virtue of Interior Silence 244

46. Virtue of Contemplation 250

Part Ten
Holy Trinity, Mold Me in Your *Adoremus* Virtues

47. Virtue of Gratitude 257

48. Virtue of Praise 262

49. Virtue of Awe 266

50. Virtue of Adoration 270

Appendix

V. References and Notes 275

Dedication

I wish to dedicate this devotional to all the wonderful people who have fed me in my spiritual journey:

My parents, Rejohn George and Christina D'Silva

All my family, friends, and parish community

Sr. Enda Mena Ryan F.M.M. and all Assuntarians

Acknowledgments

My beloved spouse, Don.

Agathians Shelter

Father Beiting Appalachian Mission Center (FBAMC)

Food for the Poor

Rescue Mission

St. Paul's Street Evangelization (SPSE)

Unbound

United Nations High Commissioner for Refugees

You, dear reader, for your openness to Christian growth

Introduction

2018. The maple tree between our house and the barn had been dying over a couple of years. It had green leaves, but they were wilting away. Knowing very little about trees, I asked my husband, Don, "Is it because it is on a slope? Is it carrying a virus? If it is, will it spread to all our other trees? Let's chop it down, honey." Much conversation, but both of us just let it be.

A few days later, it was Labor Day. Just before taking a siesta, I spent some time in prayer, seeking the Lord's counsel and direction in writing a devotional on virtues. My second book, *Holy Rivers of God, Heal Me!*, which addressed healing of different root sins and vices, was already published. I did not want this just to be my will, but His will. After all, there were many books already out there that explore virtues. *Show me that this is really Your will, Lord.*

I got up from my nap due to a ruckus of winds and rain. Looking out of the window, I realized that either a mini-tornado or straight wind was taking place. I called Don who told me that he was in the barn. "You had better stay put, Don. It is pretty bad out there," I warned him.

Meanwhile, I settled at my work space and brainstormed (no pun intended) on all the Christian virtues I could think of. In less than seven minutes, the

Holy Spirit inspired me to jot down as many virtues as I knew based on Christian sacred tradition.

When I had finished writing down fifty virtues, so had the winds stopped and the rain receded. Don and I went to meet each other between the house and the barn. Lo and behold, the maple tree was on the ground. It had snapped at the base. An *Act of God*, I thought, to uproot so as to plant. I felt that God had answered my prayer.

So dear reader, let virtues take root now and grow within your heart, body, soul, and spirit as you pray through this devotional. Let the Holy Spirit inform you of a given virtue through *Sacred Tradition*, particularly through the Catechism and Word of God, and scholarly writers who seek to define and explicate each virtue. Let the *Christian saints, martyrs, and holy ones' sayings* dwell richly in your soul as you ponder upon them and imitate them in holiness.

Let the recommended *prayers for each virtue* become an intercession to the Holy Trinity to change you in His grace from glory to glory. Let the *fifty-day virtues journal* (the companion book) be your soul's work space to jot down insights and desires for growth in a given virtue. In *humility*, the greatest virtue, love God above all, and be a blessing unto others as you grow in Him!

May God bless you, abundantly!   *Annet O'Mara*

Disclaimers:

The "I" in these prayers does not refer to the author, nor does it presume or imply anything about a particular reader. If a given prayer does not directly apply to you, insert the name of a person or group of people for whom you wish to earnestly pray.

Some anecdotes are non-fictional and refer to real people whose permission to use has been granted. Other short stories are purely fictional, based on universal themes chosen to resonate with the reader. It is the author's intent that these illustrations will add context and personal inspiration.

Avalanche of Grace!

Day 1 – Virtue of Faith

Faith is the theological virtue by which we believe in God and believe all that he has said and revealed to us, and that Holy Church proposes for our belief, because he is truth itself. By faith "man freely commits his entire self to God."[78] For this reason the believer seeks to know and do God's will. "The righteous shall live by faith. 'Living faith' work[s] through charity."[79]

The gift of faith remains in one who has not sinned against it.[80] But "faith apart from works is dead":[81] when it is deprived of hope and love, faith does not fully unite the believer to Christ and does not make him a living member of his Body.

The disciple of Christ must not only keep the faith and live on it, but also profess it, confidently bear witness to it, and spread it: "All however must be prepared to confess Christ before men and to follow him along the way of the Cross, amidst the persecutions which the Church never lacks."[82] Service of and witness to the faith are necessary for salvation: "So everyone who acknowledges me before men, I also will acknowledge before my Father who is in heaven; but whoever denies me before men, I also will deny before my Father who is in heaven."[83]

(Catechism of the Catholic Church 1812-1816)

Avalanche of Grace!

Day 1 – Reflections on the Virtue of Faith

"My Lord and My God" — St. Thomas the Apostle.

"Faith is to believe what you do not see; the reward of this faith is to see what you believe" — St. Augustine of Hippo.

"May you trust God that you are exactly where you are meant to be" — St. Therese of Lisieux.

"The most beautiful act of faith is the one made in darkness, in sacrifice, and with extreme effort" — St. Pio of Pietrelcina.

"In the light of faith, you see things quite differently"
— St. John Baptist de la Salle.

"It is faith that delivers through the Blood of Christ"
— St. Ambrose of Milan.

"To one who has faith, no explanation is necessary. To one without faith, no explanation is possible"
— St. Thomas Aquinas.

Avalanche of Grace!

Day 1 – Prayer for the Virtue of Faith

Read God's Word: Mark 10: 46-52

O Father, all faith stems from Your love for me!
O Jesus, Son of David, have pity on me!
O Holy Spirit, increase my faith in things I do not see!

Jesus, I believe that You are the Son of God and Mary.
Jesus, I believe that You are my Savior,
my Redeemer, and my Healer.
Jesus, I believe that you love me
no matter what my past is.
Jesus, I believe You died on the Cross for my sins.
Jesus, I believe I shall see You face to face in heaven.

Jesus, I believe in Your Real Presence in the Eucharist.
Jesus, I trust and receive Your radiations of love
in my body, spirit, and soul.
Jesus, please remove the spiritual scales from my eyes.

O Father, I run to Your embrace many times a day!
O Jesus, I trust in Your mercy for my lack of faith!
O Holy Spirit, infuse more seeds of faith in me!

Day 1 – A Story of Virtuous Faith

When Jacinta was about twenty, her friend Ela, a 35 year old Brahmin Hindu, told her that her five-year old daughter, Dayita, had renal failure and would need to go into surgery. Jacinta was told that little Dayita might also need a kidney. Jacinta offered both her kidney, if needed, and a prayer. She told Ela that Jesus could heal her daughter if she believed in His power to do so.

Ela shared with Jacinta that as a Brahmin Hindu, she believed that Jesus is the God who heals. So Jacinta connected her with her own mom who was part of a charismatic prayer group. With Jacinta's mom, Ela and Dayita went to a prayer meeting to be prayed over. Jesus, our Savior and Healer, heard the cry of a mother's heart and the community of believers, and healed Dayita miraculously over the next few days. Her doctors confirmed this and reported that she no longer needed a kidney transplant. Ela praised Jesus!

Later in life, Dayita became a medical doctor. Praise God!

Jesus: I love you, my beloved. I am Your Healer. I am Your Savior. I am the God of all peoples and nations. Trust in Me, in My designs, in My plans, and in My will for you.

I: Jesus, I Love You and I Trust in You! I believe You can completely heal me and those whom I love!

Avalanche of Grace!

Day 2 – Virtue of Hope

Hope is the theological virtue by which we desire the kingdom of heaven and eternal life as our happiness, placing our trust in Christ's promises and relying not on our own strength, but on the help of the grace of the Holy Spirit. "Let us hold fast the confession of our hope without wavering, for he who promised is faithful."[84] "The Holy Spirit . . . he poured out upon us richly through Jesus Christ our Savior, so that we might be justified by his grace and become heirs in hope of eternal life."[85]

The virtue of hope responds to the aspiration to happiness which God has placed in the heart of every man; it takes up the hopes that inspire men's activities and purifies them so as to order them to the Kingdom of heaven; it keeps man from discouragement; it sustains him during times of abandonment; it opens up his heart in expectation of eternal beatitude. Buoyed up by hope, he is preserved from selfishness and led to the happiness that flows from charity.

Christian hope takes up and fulfills the hope of the chosen people which has its origin and model in the *hope of Abraham*, who was blessed abundantly by the promises of God fulfilled in Isaac, and who was purified by the test of the sacrifice.[86] "Hoping against hope, he believed, and thus became the father of many nations."[87]

Christian hope unfolds from the beginning of Jesus' preaching in the proclamation of the *beatitudes*. The beatitudes raise our hope toward heaven as the new Promised Land; they trace the path that leads through the trials that await the disciples of Jesus. But through the merits of Jesus Christ and of his Passion, God keeps us in the "hope that does not disappoint."[88] Hope is the "sure and steadfast anchor of the soul . . . that enters . . . where Jesus has gone as a forerunner on our behalf."[89] Hope is also a weapon that protects us in the struggle of salvation: "Let us . . . put on the breastplate of faith and charity, and for a helmet the hope of salvation."[90] It affords us joy even under trial: "Rejoice in your hope, be patient in tribulation."[91] Hope is expressed and nourished in prayer, especially in the Our Father, the summary of everything that hope leads us to desire.

We can therefore hope in the glory of heaven promised by God to those who love him and do his will.[92] In every circumstance, each one of us should hope, with the grace of God, to persevere "to the end"[93] and to obtain the joy of heaven, as God's eternal reward for the good works accomplished with the grace of Christ. In hope, the Church prays for "all men to be saved."[94] She longs to be united with Christ, her Bridegroom, in the glory of heaven:

> Hope, O my soul, hope. You know neither the day nor the hour. Watch carefully, for everything

passes quickly, even though your impatience makes doubtful what is certain, and turns a very short time into a long one. Dream that the more you struggle, the more you prove the love that you bear your God, and the more you will rejoice one day with your Beloved, in a happiness and rapture that can never end.[95]

(Catechism of the Catholic Church 1817-1821)

Avalanche of Grace!

Day 2 – Reflections on the Virtue of Hope

"Blessed are they who hope in the Lord" —Psalm 1:1.

"The cross means that there is no shipwreck without hope; there is no dark without dawn; nor storm without haven"
—St. John Paul II.

"Wait upon the Lord; be faithful to His commandments; He will elevate your hope, and put you in possession of His Kingdom. Wait upon Him patiently; wait upon Him by avoiding all sin. He will come, doubt it not; and in the approaching day of His visitation, which will be that of your death and His judgment, He will Himself crown your holy hope. Place all your hope in the Heart of Jesus; it is a safe asylum; for he who trusts in God is sheltered and protected by His mercy. To this firm hope, join the practice of virtue, and even in this life you will begin to taste the ineffable joys of Paradise"
—Saint Bernard of Clairvaux.

"Even when alone, be cheerful, remembering that you are always in the sight of angels" —St. Therese of Lisieux.

Avalanche of Grace!

Day 2 – Prayer for the Virtue of Hope

Read God's Word: Romans 8: 18-25

O Father, all hope is a silent waiting upon You!
O Jesus, waters of salvation, I thirst for You!
O Holy Spirit, I groan for creation to be renewed!

Jesus, you are my hope.
Water my dry ground with confidence and courage
in moments of self-doubt and timidity.
Holy Spirit, strengthen my will
to be hope for the hopeless
by how I think, say, and act
in the very little things I do for You and all.
May my words be consoling, and my presence,
Your silent Presence.

Holy God, I hope in eternal life when I shall see you face-to-face. I have faith and hope that even as these two virtues pass, love remains forever.

O Father, I am blessed in Your total love for me!
O Jesus, I receive your grace of hope in abundance!
O Holy Spirit, deepen my hope in areas I yet not know!

Avalanche of Grace!

Day 2 – A Story of Virtuous Hope

Nate and Lina were ecstatic when their child, David, was born. His Chinese name is "A New Song." Both Nate and Lina were told about three months before that David would have a rare heart disease. They had brought their pain to the Joneses, who prayed with them. The Joneses encouraged them to be constant in their hope, love, and joy. Many other Christians prayed with them, too, asking the Lord to heal David. They reminded Nate and Lina that Jesus has power over the disease. Nate and Lina started sharing their faith amidst their trials. They believed that David, as with every child, was perfect in God's eyes – *his heart is exactly how God created it!*

Two days before Lina's scheduled induced labor, Nate and Lina decided to cancel the procedure. They trusted in the Lord to trigger the delivery at the right time. Sure enough, Lina went into labor the next day. David was born but still needed heart surgery. Yet each new medical challenge only deepened Nate and Lina's faith as they placed their hope in the Lord. Now, a feisty little David brings hope to all with his smile.

Jesus: I am singing a new song in Your heart — of hope, joy, and love. Do you hear it? Let our hearts sing!

I: Jesus, I want to sing in You. Holy Spirit teach me the words. I need a total renewal of spirit and soul in You.

Day 3 – Virtue of Charity

Charity is the theological virtue by which we love God above all things for his own sake, and our neighbor as ourselves for the love of God.

Jesus makes charity the *new commandment*.[96] By loving his own "to the end,"[97] he makes manifest the Father's love which he receives. By loving one another, the disciples imitate the love of Jesus which they themselves receive. Whence Jesus says: "As the Father has loved me, so have I loved you; abide in my love." And again: "This is my commandment, that you love one another as I have loved you."[98]

Fruit of the Spirit and fullness of the Law, charity keeps the *commandments* of God and his Christ: "Abide in my love. If you keep my commandments, you will abide in my love."[99]

Christ died out of love for us, while we were still "enemies."[100] The Lord asks us to love as he does, even our *enemies*, to make ourselves the neighbor of those farthest away, and to love children and the poor as Christ himself.[101]

The Apostle Paul has given an incomparable depiction of charity: "charity is patient and kind, charity is not jealous or boastful; it is not arrogant or rude. Charity does not insist on its own way; it is not irritable or resentful; it does not rejoice at wrong, but rejoices in the right. Charity bears all things, believes all things, hopes all things, endures all things."[102]

"If I . . . have not charity," says the Apostle, "I am nothing." Whatever my privilege, service, or even virtue, "if I . . . have not charity, I gain nothing."[103] Charity is superior to all the virtues. It is the first of the theological virtues: "So faith, hope, charity abide, these three. But *the greatest of these is charity.*"[104]

The practice of all the virtues is animated and inspired by charity, which "binds everything together in perfect harmony";[105] it is the *form of the virtues*; it articulates and orders them among themselves; it is the source and the goal of their Christian practice. Charity upholds and purifies our human ability to love, and raises it to the supernatural perfection of divine love.

The practice of the moral life animated by charity gives to the Christian the spiritual freedom of the children of God. He no longer stands before God as a slave, in servile fear, or as a mercenary looking for wages, but as a son responding to the love of him who "first loved us":[106] If we turn away from evil out of fear of punishment, we are in the position of slaves. If we pursue the enticement of wages, . . . we resemble mercenaries. Finally if we obey for the sake of the good itself and out of love for him who commands . . . we are in the position of children.[107]

The *fruits* of charity are joy, peace, and mercy; charity demands beneficence and fraternal correction; it is benevolence; it fosters reciprocity and remains disinterested and generous; it is friendship and communion: Love is itself the fulfillment of all our works. There is the goal; that is why we run: we run toward it, and once we reach it, in it we shall find rest.[108]

(Catechism of the Catholic Church 1822-1829)

Avalanche of Grace!

Day 3 – Reflections on the Virtue of Charity

"No one has greater love than this, to lay down one's life for one's friends" —John 15:13.

"The Eucharist is the supreme proof of the love of Jesus… after that, there is heaven itself" —St. Peter Julian Eymard.

"It is not enough to love, people have to feel that they are loved" —St. John Bosco.

"Love, to be real, must empty us of self"
—St. Teresa of Calcutta.

"The measure of love is to love without measure"
—St. Francis de Sales.

"I prefer the monotony of obscure sacrifices to all the ecstasies. To pick up a pin for love can convert a soul"
—St. Therese of Lisieux.

"At the end of life, we shall be judged by love"
—St. John of the Cross.

Avalanche of Grace!

Day 3 – Prayer for the Virtue of Charity

Read God's Word: 1 Corinthians 13

O Father, all real love springs from Your bosom!
O Jesus, Sacred Heart who was pierced for my sins!
O Holy Spirit, true love of the Father and Jesus!

Father, Son and Holy Spirit,
the quintessence of charity,
the perfect family of unity,
the river waters of love and mercy,
refresh the waters of charity in me to become
streams of grace to love You and others more.

Holy Trinity, even if Your other graces cease,
I simply ask Your love to be poured out on me
to love others in lowly ways.
Let me suffer with and for others
as a sweet and humble offering to You.

O Father, I wish to forgive all as You have me!
O Jesus, I thank you for loving my wounds!
O Holy Spirit, lovingly retouch my wounds to love!

Day 3 – A Story of Virtuous Love

"'Til death do us apart" finds total expression in Deb's life. Her husband had suffered a stroke the year before. At this time, she takes care of him at home. Now and again, folks ask her why she does not place her spouse in a nursing home. Deb explains that she finds true peace in taking care of him in their home and placing both their needs in Jesus' heart, one day at a time.

Deb knows no boundaries in her total self-giving love and sacrifice for her husband. She loves until the end, just as Jesus loves us into eternity. No greater love is there than to lay down one's life for a spouse, a child, a family member, friend, stranger, or enemy.

Jesus: My Child, will you open your heart like a bowl and receive from My overflow of love? I will direct My love into you and through all the chambers of your Heart if you but let Me. I am in your family, friends, neighbors, strangers, enemies, the poor, the outcast and unlovable, too, wanting to be loved.

I: Jesus, I am ready to open the bowl of my heart for You. Pour out Your love and directives through every chamber of my heart onto others so that they may feel your love.

Avalanche of Grace!

Day 4 – Virtue of Prudence

Cardinal Virtues

Virtue is a habitual and firm disposition to do good.

The human virtues are stable dispositions of the intellect and the will that govern our acts, order our passions, and guide our conduct in accordance with reason and faith. They can be grouped around the four cardinal virtues: prudence, justice, fortitude, and temperance.

Prudence disposes the practical reason to discern, in every circumstance, our true good and to choose the right means for achieving it.

(Catechism of the Catholic Church 1833-1835)

Virtue of Prudence

The virtue of prudence directs all the other virtues. For prudence is the ability to recognize what is right. After all, someone who wants to lead a good life must know what the "good" is and recognize its worth. Like the merchant in the gospel "who, on finding one pearl of great value, went and sold all that he had and bought it" (Matthew 13:46). Only the prudent person can apply the virtues of justice, fortitude, and moderation so as to do good *(YOUCAT, 173)*.

Day 4 – Reflections on the Virtue of Prudence

"Plans are made in human hearts, but from the Lord comes the tongue's response. All one's ways are pure in one's own eyes, but the measurer of motives is the Lord's"
—*Proverbs 16: 1-2.*

"Virtue without prudence is not virtue at all. We should often pray to the Holy Spirit for the gift of prudence. Prudence consists in discretion, rational reflection, and courageous resolution. The final decision is always up to us"
—*St. Faustina Kowalska.*

"Don't judge without having heard both sides. Even persons who think themselves as virtuous very easily forget this elementary rule of prudence" —*St. Josemaria Escriva.*

"Act today in such a way that you need not blush tomorrow"
—*St. John Bosco.*

"Silence is the cross on which we must crucify our ego"
—*St. Seraphim of Sarov.*

Avalanche of Grace!

Day 4 – Prayer for the Virtue of Prudence

Read God's Word: Proverbs 8: 1-31

O Father, before the world began, prudence was!
O Jesus, Son of Wisdom and Prudence!
O Holy Spirit, Giver of Wisdom and Counsel!

Endue me, Holy Trinity, with:
right Godly thinking that I may be prudent,
correct Spirit-filled counsel that I may act wisely,
and, a teachable spirit that I may advance in wisdom.

I ask for the gift of silence to help me restrain
harsh words, rash judgments or actions.

O Holy Trinity, I enlist your grace in all Your plans
for me and others for whom I pray.
I unite my thoughts and plans to You.
I entrust them to You.

O Father, I love that prudence is as old as You!
O Jesus, by Your Cross, enliven prudence in me!
O Holy Spirit, let prudence guard all virtues in me!

Day 4 – A Story of Virtuous Prudence

Logan and Linda were ostracized, cut off, insulted, and thrown out of their own church by the pastor for merely offering counsel about troubling situations that were born of territorialism and jealousy.

Prudence dictated that Logan and Linda remain silent in the face of taunts and insults. They understood that prudence was there before the clods of the world came to be and how it flows from the heart of God, whereas envy and jealousy are created by the evil one to promote discord.

Logan and Linda forgave their former pastor, praying everyday that the Lord would just shower His blessings upon him and the flock they were unjustly cut off from.

God blessed Logan and Linda again with streams of grace and led them on a new path in accordance with His Will. He used them effectively at a different church, where His spirit brought them a great sense of peace.

Jesus: I want you, My Child, to reflect prudence in your speech and actions. When you do so, you reflect My dwelling in you, and you in Me.

I: I wish to be pruned to become prudent in my words and behavior. Grace me with Your Holy Indwelling.

Avalanche of Grace!

Day 5 – Virtue of Justice

Justice consists in the firm and constant will to give God and neighbor their due.
(Catechism of the Catholic Church 1836)

The guiding principle of justice is: "To each his due." A child with a disability and a highly gifted child must be encouraged in different ways so that each may fulfill his potential. Justice is concerned with equity and longs to see people get that to which they are entitled. We must allow justice to govern our relations with God also and give him what is his: our love and worship (*YOUCAT* 173-174).

Avalanche of Grace!

Day 5 – Reflections on the Virtue of Justice

"Learn to do good. Make justice your aim: redress the wronged, hear the orphan's plea, defend the widow"
—Isaiah 1:17.

"Rather let justice surge like waters, and righteousness like an unfailing stream" —Amos 5:24.

"You have been told, O mortal, what is good, and what the LORD requires of you: only to do justice and to love goodness, and to walk humbly with your God" —Micah 6:8.

"If you have two shirts in your closet, one belongs to you and the other to the man with no shirt" —St. Ambrose of Milan.

"Charity is no substitute for justice withheld"
—St. Augustine of Hippo.

"I make myself a leper with the lepers to gain all for Jesus Christ" —St. Damien of Molokai.

"Let us pray, bear little crosses, and greatly love the souls of all our neighbors without exception, friends or enemies"
—St. Maximilian Kolbe.

Avalanche of Grace!

Day 5 – Prayer for the Virtue of Justice

Read God's Word: Romans 12

O Father, who is Just in loving all!
O Jesus, Lover of Justice and Mercy!
O Holy Spirit, who gives of the One Spirit!

Holy Trinity, grant me a firm and constant will to
do justice, love goodness and walk humbly in God.

I desire to love my neighbors fairly.
Show me, Holy Spirit, how to touch their lives
with my gifts of presence, listening, and sharing.

O Jesus, let justice reign in all hearts!
You have fed me with Your Body and Blood.
May I, in turn, feed the hungry and the poor.
You healed me in Your Body and Blood.
May I, in turn, care for the sick and the suffering.

O Father, grace me to love all your children fairly!
O Jesus, Atonement of All Iniquity, teach me to be equitable!
O Holy Spirit, train me day by day to be fair to all!

Avalanche of Grace!

Day 5 – A Story of Virtuous Justice

Lisa expressed to an elder Christian that she was going to be out of a job shortly. The elder whispered to her: "Let me ask you a question. Do you tithe your income to the Lord?" Lisa said, "Not more than a couple of dollars when the basket comes around." The elder just smiled and said, "Think about it. When you bless Him from your need, He will bless you abundantly. God loves a cheerful giver."

Lisa started tithing to God 2% of her income, and later increased it to 5%, and then 10% over the course of her career. Then, Lisa blessed some immediate family members who were in need, and also sponsored children in developing countries through *Food for the Poor* and *Unbound*, as God continued to meet her own needs. While volunteering at the *Rescue Mission* in the United States and the *Agathians Shelter* in Malaysia, she realized that often true heartfelt gratitude overflows from the most vulnerable – the poor and orphans.

Lisa never got to thank the elder for the wise, biblical advice but believes that her friend is now interceding for her, the poor and orphans in heaven.

Jesus: I want you to know, My Child, that when you show mercy to God and all, without exception, you are being just and fair to My Heart as well as My other children.

I: Show me who else needs justice and kindness!

Day 6 – Virtue of Fortitude

Fortitude ensures firmness in difficulties and constancy in the pursuit of the good.

(Catechism of the Catholic Church 1837)

YOUCAT scholars, drawing on the *Catechism of the Catholic Church* paragraphs 1809 and 1837, clarify this virtue as follows: "Someone who practices fortitude perseveres in his commitment to do good. [Once] he has recognized it, even if in the extreme case he must sacrifice even his own life for it" (174).

Avalanche of Grace!

Day 6 – Reflections on the Virtue of Fortitude

"I command you: be strong and steadfast! Do not fear nor be dismayed, for the LORD, your God, is with you wherever you go" —Joshua 1:9.

"The LORD is my light and my salvation; whom should I fear? The LORD is my life's refuge; of whom should I be afraid?" —Psalm 27:1.

"Hope has two beautiful daughters: their names are anger and courage. Anger that things are the way they are. Courage to make them the way they ought to be" —St. Augustine of Hippo.

"The principal act of courage is to endure and withstand dangers doggedly rather than to attack them" —St. Thomas Aquinas.

"The gift of fortitude is asked for, when He says: 'Give us this day our daily bread.' Bread strengthens the heart of a [person]" —St. Bonaventure di Fidanza.

"Ponder the fact that God made you a gardener to root out vice and to plant virtue" —St. Catherine of Siena.

Avalanche of Grace!

Day 6 – Prayer for the Virtue of Fortitude

Read God's Word: 2 Timothy 1: 1-18

O Father, Fount of fortitude and courage!
O Jesus, Lamb who submitted to the Father's will!
O Holy Spirit, Spirit of patience and perseverance!

Holy Trinity, I ask for Your grace to defend my faith,
no matter the humiliations and sufferings.

O Holy Spirit, plant seeds of fortitude
in me to speak the truth and not be afraid.
Water my arid soul.
Give me the strength to die for my faith.
Help me fight to protect human life in all its stages.

O Holy Trinity, raise up courageous Christians,
after Your own Heart, who will burn with zeal
for Your Body, the Church, and for all souls.

O Father, let me be gallant for You who loves Me!
O Jesus, like Mary, I want to stand at Your cross!
O Holy Spirit, give me the courage to defend You!

Day 6 – A Story of Virtuous Fortitude

"White cars are easier to come by," said the car salesman. Agnes looked at his family pictures on the wall behind his desk. She asked him if one of the girls in the family portrait was the daughter he had referenced, the one who had "inherited" the family's white sedan. "Yes," he said, "that's *her*, and she was unplanned. She is my pride and my joy." He could not have imagined any option other than keeping her, given his Christian roots.

"Have you heard of the movie titled *Unplanned?*" Agnes asked. "No," he said. As they talked, he mentioned that he knew of Abby Johnson, the subject of the movie.

Johnson left Planned Parenthood after she had watched the ultrasound of a baby being aborted. She was horrified and grief-stricken by what she witnessed and sought the help of *Forty Days for Life* to change her stance from then on and to speak up for life.

God is grateful to the salesman for letting his unplanned daughter live. If only all would accept His gifts, especially the precious gift of life.

Jesus: My Child, Your mom defied all odds to have and keep you. Will you keep Me in every conceived baby?

I: Yes. Thank You for knitting me in my mom's womb.

Avalanche of Grace!

Day 7 – Virtue of Temperance

Temperance moderates the attraction of the pleasures of the senses and provides balance in the use of created goods.

>*(Catechism of the Catholic Church 1838)*

YOUCAT scholars, drawing on the *Catechism of the Catholic Church* paragraphs 1809 and 1838, explicate this virtue as follows:

> Moderation is a virtue because immoderate behavior proves to be a destructive force in all areas of life.
>
> Someone who is immoderate abandons himself to the rule of his impulses, offends others by his inordinate desires, and harms himself. In the New Testament, words like "sobriety" and "discretion" stand for "moderation." *(174)*

Day 7 – Reflections on the Virtue of Temperance

"Let us conduct ourselves properly as in the day, — not in orgies and drunkenness, not in promiscuity and licentiousness, not in rivalry and jealousy. But put on the Lord Jesus Christ, and make no provision for the desires of the flesh" —Romans 13:13-14.

"Temperance is simply a disposition of the minds which binds passion" —St. Thomas Aquinas.

"Join humility to temperance, for the one without the other is useless" —St. John Climacus.

"Temperance is love surrendering itself wholly to Him who is its object; courage is love bearing all things gladly for the sake of Him who is its object; justice is love serving Him only who is its object, and therefore rightly ruling; prudence is love making wise decision between what hinders and what helps itself" —St. Augustine of Hippo.

"You wish to reform the world? Reform yourself; otherwise, your efforts will be in vain" —St. Ignatius of Loyola.

"If you wish to go to extremes let it be in sweetness, patience, humility, and charity" —St. Philip Neri.

Avalanche of Grace!

Day 7 – Prayer for the Virtue of Temperance

Read God's Word: 2 Peter 1: 3-11

O Father, who loves me passionately!
O Jesus, whose sacrifice teaches me self-denial!
O Holy Spirit, Spirit who directs my soul!

Holy Trinity, I ask to be emptied
of all desires and cravings of the flesh.
Renew in me a spirit of prayer, fasting, and abstinence
to bind disordered appetites and passions.
Temper all my wants.

O Holy Trinity, I submit all my will, intentions,
and motivations to Your Will. Help me control
my thoughts, words, and actions for the good of all.

O Holy Trinity, I am only free in Your school
of discipline that teaches me to love You and others.

O Father, I desire to love You first and eternally!
O Jesus, help me renounce all for Your sake!
O Holy Spirit, I receive Your gift of self-control!

Day 7 – A Story of Virtuous Temperance

Bill finally realized that his excessive fixation on texting and checking his phone brought about his suffering. His girl-friend broke up with him on *Facebook* by changing her status. "Why did she do that?" he kept asking. Bill went spiraling from hurt to anger to drinking bouts, depression, and a suicide attempt all within a couple of weeks.

A friend, Edgar, visited Bill and asked him, "Do you not know that the Father loves you and created you in His own image? He wants you to know that you are precious in His eyes. Social media can cause some to forget who they are. Egos thrive through the many selfies folks promote. Many have lost a sense of propriety in relationships. Get on an even keel with the Father. He truly loves you and will heal you."

Bill listened to Edgar and let God love him. Once found by Him, his Father Forever, who could satisfy his thirst, he sought after Jesus' ways. With the Holy Spirit's wisdom, Bill started forming holy and lasting relationships. He also changed his social media habits to spend only about fifteen minutes daily online.

Jesus: "My child, I am here. Pour your heart out to Me."

I: "Yes. I am sorry for neglecting You. I do not wish to lose You, Jesus, my All in all."

Avalanche of Grace!

Day 8 – Virtue of Poverty

St. John Chrysostom vigorously recalls this: "Not to enable the poor to share in our goods is to steal from them and deprive them of life. The goods we possess are not ours, but theirs."[239] "The demands of justice must be satisfied first of all; that which is already due in justice is not to be offered as a gift of charity":[240]

> When we attend to the needs of those in want, we give them what is theirs, not ours. More than performing works of mercy, we are paying a debt of justice.[241]

(Catechism of the Catholic Church 2446)

Avalanche of Grace!

Day 8 – Reflections on the Virtue of Poverty

"Blessed are the poor in spirit, for theirs is the kingdom of heaven" —Matthew 5: 3.

"The soul hungers for God and nothing but God can satiate it" —St. Jean Marie Vianney.

"Build yourself a cell in your heart and retire there to pray" —St. Catherine of Siena.

"Don't let aridity distress you. Your devotion will come back when you least expect it" —St. Teresa of Avila.

"Being unwanted, unloved, uncared for, forgotten by everybody, I think that is a much greater hunger, a much greater poverty, than the person who has nothing to eat" —St. Teresa of Calcutta.

"If you cannot find Christ in the beggar at the church door, you will not find Him in the chalice" —St. John Chrysostom.

"The poor and the sick are the heart of God. In serving them, we serve Jesus Christ" —St. Camillus de Lellis.

"Let us go to Jesus. He is all alone and hardly anyone thinks of Him. Poor Jesus!" —St. Gemma Galgani.

Avalanche of Grace!

Day 8 – Prayer for the Virtue of Poverty

Read God's Word: Mark 14: 3-9

O Father, Father of the poor, orphans, and widows!
O Jesus, Friend, Healer, and Savior of the poor!
O Holy Spirit, whose first ministry is to the poor!

Only You, Holy Spirit, can satisfy the thirsty.
Only You, Holy Spirit, can comfort the poor.
Only You, Holy Spirit, can care for the vulnerable.
Only You, Holy Spirit, can heal the needy.

Fill my own spiritual thirst, and touch my poverty, vulnerability, and neediness with Your love!
Then, use me to bring others to love You deeply.

Jesus, You have said, "Blessed are the poor in spirit.
The kingdom of heaven is theirs." May I, too,
be saved and humbly counted among the poor.

O Father, I thirst for your fatherhood over my soul!
O Jesus, help me console and serve You in all!
O Holy Spirit, help me model Your giving — freely!

Avalanche of Grace!

Day 8 – A Story of Virtuous Poverty

I watched both my father Georgie and mother Christina offer monetary gifts, food, or a place to stay to any relative who needed help. It was not as if we were rich, but my parents just knew in their hearts that God's blessings had to be shared with one and all.

After my father died at the age of 48, I watched my mom expand her gift of giving by providing three of her children a college education so that they could learn "to fish" for life. She also visited the sick and dying to bring them Holy Communion and to offer a prayer of healing. Some of the sick were physically healed by Jesus and lived for many years after.

In her 80's, mom shared with our family how as a child growing up in India, she had seen a lady without any clothes on her street. So mom went home to get a blanket to put over the poor naked woman.

Jesus: "My child, do not be afraid to feed and clothe Me in the poor and the naked. I trust in your mercy."

I: "I want to serve You, Jesus, in the poor and naked."

Avalanche of Grace!

Day 9 – Virtue of Mourning

The bodies of the dead must be treated with respect and charity, in faith and hope of the Resurrection. The burial of the dead is a corporal work of mercy;[92] it honors the children of God, who are temples of the Holy Spirit.

This teaching [on the final purification] is also based on the practice of prayer for the dead, already mentioned in Sacred Scripture: "Therefore Judas Maccabeus made atonement for the dead that they might be delivered from their sin."[609] From the beginning the Church has honored the memory of the dead and offered prayers in suffrage for them, above all the Eucharistic sacrifice, so that, thus purified, they may attain the beatific vision of God.[610] The Church also commends almsgiving, indulgences, and works of penance undertaken on behalf of the dead:

Let us help and commemorate them. If Job's sons were purified by their father's sacrifice, why would we doubt that our offerings for the dead bring them some consolation? Let us not hesitate to help those who have died and to offer our prayers for them.[611]

(Catechism of the Catholic Church 2300, 1032)

Avalanche of Grace!

Day 9 – Reflections on the Virtue of Mourning

"Blessed are they who mourn, for they will be comforted"
—Matthew 5: 4.

"The world's thy ship and not thy home" —St. Therese of Lisieux.

"Like our Lady, remain at the Cross of Christ, and you will never be deprived of comfort"—St. Pio of Pietrelcina.

"A single Mass offered for a person while alive may be worth more than a thousand offered for the person after death"
—St. Anselm of Canterbury.

"When you are weary of praying and do not receive, consider how many times you have heard a poor man calling and have not listened to him"—St John Chrysostom.

"Apart from the Cross, there is no other ladder by which we may get to heaven"—St. Rose of Lima.

"The best way to prepare for death is to spend every day of life as though it was your last"—St. Philip Neri.

"If all were to know how beautiful Jesus is and how loving He is, they would all die of love. And yet, how is it that He is so little loved?"—St. Gemma Galgani.

Avalanche of Grace!

Day 9 – Prayer for the Virtue of Mourning

Read God's Word: Luke 7: 11-17

O Father, Father, You Sacrificed Your Beloved Son!
O Jesus, Consoler of Martha and Mary!
O Holy Spirit, Comforter of those who mourn!

Gift me with your grace to mourn with those:
who have sacrificed their child for our country;
who have experienced the loss of family members;
who have lost some physical or mental capacity;
who are on the bed of pain or terminally ill;
who have suffered loss of livelihood or property;
who have been stripped of their dignity;
who have lost a baby or cannot have one;
who are separated from family due to war;
who carry heavy burdens for family members;
and, who are sick or dying alone on the streets.

O Father, comfort Your people with hope!
O Jesus, unite all those who mourn under Your Cross!
O Holy Spirit, O Comforter, let them rest in You!

Day 9 – A Story of Virtuous Mourning

Post-surgery. Knowing that his father was slipping away, my spouse Don, with his mom and brother, recited the Divine Mercy Chaplet. After they had finished, Don made the sign of the cross on his father's head. As Mom kissed his forehead, Dad's weak heartbeat faded to silence. For many months, as Don grieved his father's passing, he found much comfort in reciting a Divine Mercy Chaplet every day for his father and all holy souls.

Memories of his father bring more comfort to Don and put a smile on all our faces. *Who served cabbage instead of lettuce for salad when mom was away? Who had to own up to getting dad's car in an accident? Who gave counsel on how to build homes and do home repairs, until the unfortunate fall that caused a hip fracture and took his life?* Recently, after accidentally cutting his wrist with a pair of pruning shears, Don received seven stitches. In a pensive moment, he shared, *"Dad used to take out my stitches."* [Not to be tried at home, his beloved advises, as Don's attempt to do this on his own was less than optimal.]

Jesus: "My child, listen to the hurt and pain of those who mourn. Offer them My comforting grace!"

I: "Jesus, help me listen to comfort those who mourn."

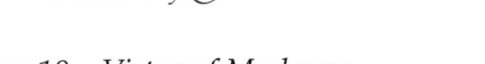

Day 10 – Virtue of Meekness

The irony is that meekness, indeed a virtue, is the one virtue above all that allows us to remain ourselves in the midst of adversity. It allows us to maintain self-possession when adversity strikes, rather than be possessed by the adversity itself.

Meekness is more synonymous with empowerment than it is with weakness because, as St. Thomas Aquinas wrote, meekness makes a man self-possessed. Dionysius has told us that Moses, surely no milquetoast, was deemed worthy of the divine apparition on account of his great meekness. According to St. Hilary, Christ dwells in us by our meekness of soul. When we are overcome by anger, we lose that sense of ourselves that allows God to dwell within us. Anger excludes God; meekness invites His presence.

Since meekness is self-possession in the face of adversity, it enables a person to do good in response to evil. Meekness is not cowardliness, timidity, or servility; it's the power that restrains the onslaught of anger and subjects it to the order of reason. While it may be more natural to express anger when one is assaulted, meekness is the higher path. It prevents evil from completely overcoming the person who is already suffering enough from evil. Meekness prevents this suffering from advancing to the precincts of the soul, first to depression and then to despair.

(Excerpt from Donald DeMarco's *Lay Witness*.)

Avalanche of Grace!

Day 10 – Reflections on the Virtue of Meekness

"Blessed are the meek, for they will inherit the land"
— Matthew 5: 5.

"...Learn from Me, for I am meek and humble of heart..."
— Matthew 11: 29.

"Rejoice heartily, O daughter Zion, shout for joy, O daughter Jerusalem! See, your king shall come to you; a just savior is he, meek, and riding on an ass, on a colt, the foal of an ass"
—Zechariah 9: 9.

"Humility perfects us with respect to God, and meekness with respect to neighbor. ...[B]alm, which sinks deeper than any other liquid symbolizes humility, while olive oil, which always rises to the top, symbolizes meekness and mildness, which rise above all things and stand out among the virtues as the flower of charity" —St. Francis de Sales.

"Christ, the Master of Humility, manifests His truth only to the humble, and hides Himself from the proud"
—St. Vincent Ferrer.

"Humility is the only thing that no devil can imitate"
—St. John Climacus.

Avalanche of Grace!

Day 10 – Prayer for the Virtue of Meekness

Read God's Word: Isaiah 53: 1-12

O Father, Uncreated and Unchanging Father!
O Jesus, Meek and Humble of Heart before all!
O Holy Spirit, Gift of Self-possession within me!

Indwelling Trinity, increase a spirit of resilience in me when I am angered, insulted, and persecuted.

Indwelling Trinity, increase a spirit of forgiveness and holy forgetfulness in me when I have been hurt.

Indwelling Trinity, increase a spirit of goodness in me where others have not been good or kind to me.

Holy Trinity, like You, I wish to remain constant in my meekness quotient. I do not wish to lose You.

O Father, whose self-possession loves forgivingly!
O Jesus, Sacred Heart, meek and humble, mold me!
O Holy Spirit, help me guard meekness within me!

Avalanche of Grace!

Day 10 – A Story of Virtuous Meekness

Selena did not know Juana from Adam but because the Lord spoke to her and told her, "Go over to that young lady and take her hand," she obeyed and went over to Juana and just held her hand. This was at a Bible study about 25 years ago.

Yes, Juana did think, "Ok, I know these people are as crazy as they come" but she guessed that Selena herself needed to be healed so she allowed Selena to cup her hands. But Selena's gentle touch was His healing grace to Juana's pain and sorrow. Selena's reassuring words were food for the latter's soul. Only then did Juana begin to understand Jesus' meekness and gentleness – in Selena's hands, which were as soft as her heart.

Over time, Juana realized that Selena never wearied of serving the *pobre** who needed prayer. Selena would journey between California and Mexico, witnessing to Christ. Those in need also travelled from afar, seeking her out to receive a prayer for healing.

Jesus: "My Child, a meek word or gesture is gentle and kind in the face of harshness, and rudeness!"

I: "Jesus, help me be meek like the eye in the storm."

*pobre in Spanish means "poor."

Avalanche of Grace!

Day 11 – Virtue of Righteousness

The greatest good, according to our culture's primary prophets, is self-esteem, self-satisfaction. Christ shocks us by blessing dissatisfaction, not the dissatisfaction with our place in the world, not worldly ambition, the profit motive, the American Dream, hunger for glory, honor, fame, power, wealth or success, but hunger and thirst for righteousness, for sanctity — dissatisfaction with our sins, passionate thirst for a sanctity we know we do not have, and know we must have.

There is one thing in the lives of all the saints that turns us off, and cuts us off, from perhaps the single most effective evangelistic weapon in the Church's arsenal — using the lives of the saints — and that is the saints' passionate insistence that they are great sinners, and their insistent passion for holiness. It's not that we do not admire holiness; it's that we do not admire the passion for holiness, the hunger and thirst for righteousness.

What Christ blesses, we curse as fanaticism, our soft, sophisticated culture's worst insult. But this is Christ's blessing. More than a blessing, it is a requirement. It is what our Lord requires us to be in order to be his, that is, to be a saint, that is, a fanatic, to love one thing infinitely, to put all our eggs in his basket. It contains only one pearl of great price. He uses a shocking word for our Laodicean niceness: "Because you are neither hot nor cold I will spit you out of my mouth." He is content with us only if we are discontent with ourselves.

(Excerpt from Peter Kreeft's talk *"Happiness: Blessed are Those Who Hunger and Thirst for Righteousness."*)

Day 11 – Reflections on the Virtue of Righteousness

"Blessed are they who hunger and thirst for righteousness for they shall be satisfied" —Matthew 5: 6.

"The saints did not all begin well but they ended well"
—St. Jean Marie Vianney.

"The gift of grace increases as the struggle increases"
—St. Rose of Lima.

"[If] a person is seeking God, the Beloved is seeking him much more" —St. John of the Cross.

"I need nothing but God, and to lose myself in the Heart of Jesus" —St. Margaret Mary Alacoque.

"While the world changes, the cross stands firm"
—St. Bruno.

"Jesus does not ask us to give up living, but to accept a newness and a fullness of life that only He can give"
—St. John Paul II.

"He who prays most, receives most"
—St. Alphonsus Liguori.

Avalanche of Grace!

Day 11 – Prayer for the Virtue of Righteousness

Read God's Word: Genesis 7: 1-24

O Father, Righteous One who satisfies the hungry!
O Jesus, Son of Righteousness who calls sinners!
O Holy Spirit, who stirs in me a passion for God!

Give voice to my spirit and soul to be shaken out of self-satisfaction and self-sufficiency to:
stand up for the voiceless in oppressive lands;
stand up for the voiceless in mothers' wombs;
stand up for the voiceless among the poor;
stand up for the voiceless among the abused;
stand up for the voiceless among the immigrants;
stand up for the voiceless among the suffering;
and, stand up for the voiceless among the governed.

I yearn for righteous grace to reign in all hearts!

O Father, satisfy my thirst and hunger for You!
O Jesus, nourish me in Your Body and Blood!
O Holy Spirit, bless my poverty that I may do right!

Day 11 – A Story of Virtuous Righteousness

When Grace's mom, Betty, was in rehabilitation for a shoulder injury, Grace went with her to the weekly rosary recited at the facility's community room. Grace's acquaintance, Shelley, along with two ladies led the rosary. They did not just lead but they brought the residents in and later took them back to their rooms after the rosary. During prayer, the rosary ladies lovingly checked on the more seriously ill patients.

In the big room, there was a great range of pain and suffering that only Our Lord and Our Lady could fathom. Yet, there was a type of joy that filled the room among the patients for that brief half hour. They had fellowship both with the Lord and one another through a holy communion of roses, "Our Lady's Psalter."

Our Lord and Our Blessed Mother touched the residents with their love. Shelley's glow, that is, Our Lady's sweet presence, was reflected in Betty and Grace's faces and all the rose-crowners gathered there.

Jesus: "My Child, I ask for a morsel a day and a drink of water from you to feed me and quench my thirst wherever you find Me."

I: "Jesus, may I have an empty basket every evening."

Avalanche of Grace!

Day 12 – Virtue of Mercy

The 12th-century mystic St. Bernard of Clairvaux pointed out that many souls refuse to turn to the Lord because they don't know him to be a God of mercy. If people don't know God's patience, how ready God is to forgive, and how much he can heal their weaknesses, then why would they bother trying to repent? It would be too hard! Bernard explains that someone considering the possibility of turning his life around will run up against his own weaknesses. If he doesn't know God's mercy and grace, he will give up in discouragement:

"If he does not know how good God is, how kind and gentle, how willing to pardon, will not his sensually inspired reason argue with him and say: 'What are you doing? ... Your sins are too grave and too many; nothing that you do, even to stripping the skin from your flesh, can make satisfaction for them. ... A lifetime's habits are not easily conquered.' Dismayed by these and similar arguments, the unhappy man quits the struggle, not knowing how easily God's omnipotent goodness could overthrow all these obstacles."

That's why we need to lead with mercy, not just moral truth. Behind the debate you're having about some moral issue is a real person who has his own struggles with various weakness, sins, hurts and fears — a person who needs God's loving help. These souls need more than an argument about why what they're doing is wrong (moral truth). Yes, they need that, but they also need the encouraging news that they can be forgiven and healed and have a fresh start in life (mercy).

(Excerpt from Dr. Edward Sri's, "Understanding Relativism with Mercy.")

Avalanche of Grace!

Day 12 – Reflections on the Virtue of Mercy

"Blessed are the merciful for they shall be shown mercy"
—Matthew 5: 7.

"To him who still remains in this world, there is no repentance that is too late"—St. Cyprian.

"My past O Lord to Your mercy, my present to Your love, and my future to Your providence"—St. Pio of Pietrelcina.

"If something uncharitable is said in your presence, either speak in favor of the absent, or withdraw, or if possible stop the conversation"—St. Jean Marie Vianney.

"If My death on the cross does not convince you of My Love, what will?"—Jesus to St. Faustina.

"As we show mercy, we shall receive mercy. We harvest what we sow"—Blessed Fulton Sheen.

"If you can't feed a hundred people, then just feed one"
—St. Teresa of Calcutta.

"How happy am I to see myself imperfect and in need of God's mercy"—St. Therese of Lisieux.

Avalanche of Grace!

Day 12 – Prayer for the Virtue of Mercy

Read God's Word: Luke 10: 25-37

O Father, Merciful Father, who welcomes all home!
O Jesus, Heart flowing with Mercy and Charity!
O Holy Spirit, Merciful fruit of the Father and Son!

Let Your Merciful Heart be right within my heart:
when regrets of past sin well up within me;
when others' flaws remind me of my own flaws;
when others are spoken of badly or ill-treated;
when one hungry soul needs to be fed or clothed;
when souls feel that God has given up on them;
and, when souls are lost and seeking clarity of faith.

Holy Trinity, most of all, help me to be community
to the wounded, lonely, neglected, and abandoned.
I wish to follow Your Mercy's heart prints!

O Father, draw all to Your merciful embrace!
O Jesus, increase in me Your thirst for mercy!
O Holy Spirit, nudge me to where mercy cries out!

Day 12 – A Story of Virtuous Mercy

Rob and Lynn had a handsome plan. *Give brown scapulars to as many Catholics as possible in a land where Mary's habit is rarely heard of or worn.* But, the chances for giving to thirsty souls were few. Well, not until they visited a nursing home and talked to Shania who was recovering from a minor stroke. They gave her a scapular and discussed the rite for proper investiture.

As they visited, Rob and Lynn heard the painful wail of a lady repeatedly calling, "Amma!" [Mother!]. Shania told Rob and Lynn that the poor lady was suffering from terminal cancer and her only family was an adult child living abroad.

Led by the Spirit, Rob and Lynn walked over to the frail, emaciated lady. They prayed with her, and told her, "The Blessed Mother, the Mother of Jesus, is your Amma. Our Amma is with you in your pain and suffering." Then, they placed a scapular over her neck.

The lady smiled a thank you to Rob and Lynn after the Blessed Mother clothed her.

Jesus: "My Child, My Mother kept vigil as I died."

I: "Jesus, please send Your Mom to all the dying!"

Avalanche of Grace!

Day 13 – Virtue of Cleanliness of Heart

The heart is the seat of moral personality: "Out of the heart come evil thoughts, murder, adultery, fornication..."[305] The struggle against carnal covetousness entails purifying the heart and practicing temperance:

> Remain simple and innocent, and you will be like little children who do not know the evil that destroys man's life.[306]

The sixth beatitude proclaims, "Blessed are the pure in heart, for they shall see God."[307] "Pure in heart" refers to those who have attuned their intellects and wills to the demands of God's holiness, chiefly in three areas: charity;[308] chastity or sexual rectitude;[309] love of truth and orthodoxy of faith.[310] There is a connection between purity of heart, of body, and of faith:

> The faithful must believe the articles of the Creed "so that by believing they may obey God, by obeying may live well, by living well may purify their hearts, and with pure hearts may understand what they believe."[311]

The "pure in heart" are promised that they will see God face to face and be like him.[312] Purity of heart is the precondition of the vision of God. Even now it enables us to see *according* to God, to accept others as "neighbors"; it lets us perceive the human body–ours and our neighbor's–as a temple of the Holy Spirit, a manifestation of divine beauty.

(Catechism of the Catholic Church 2517 – 2520)

Day 13 – Reflections on the Virtue of Cleanliness of Heart

"Blessed are the clean of heart for they shall see God"
—Matthew 5: 8.

"A heart which is free from thoughts and affections alien to God is like a temple consecrated to the Lord, in which we can contemplate Him even in this world" —St. Thomas Aquinas.

"Purity is the lily among virtues—by it men approach to the Angels. There is no beauty without purity, and human purity is chastity" —St. Francis de Sales.

"A Christian has a union with Jesus Christ more noble, more intimate, and more perfect than the members of a human body have with their head" —St. John Eudes.

"You may stain your sword with my blood, but you will never be able to profane my body, consecrated to Christ"
—St. Agnes of God.

"He who aspires to the grace of God must be pure, with a heart as innocent as a child's. Purity of heart is to God, like a perfume, sweet, and adorable" —St. Nicholas of Flue.

"The pure soul is a beautiful rose, and the Three Persons descend from Heaven to inhale its fragrance" – St. Jean Marie Vianney.

Avalanche of Grace!

Day 13 – *Prayer for the Virtue of Cleanliness of Heart*

Read God's Word: Hebrews 10: 16-39

O Father, Author of All baptisms, You purify us!
O Jesus, Your Blood and Water save and cleanse!
O Holy Spirit, fully Present as Person in baptism!

Lord, I desire to be like You – sweet purity of God!
I desire Your Blood to sprinkle my conscience.
I desire to stay pure that I may see God even now.
I desire Your intentions to cleanse my intentions.
I desire Your Will to purify my will.
I desire Your thoughts to germinate my thoughts.
I desire Your Way to straighten my ways.

Holy Trinity, I give You the temple of my heart, soul, and body to be consecrated wholly to You!
I want Your grace that I may stay forever pure in You!

O Father, I am Your Child! I know Whose I am!
O Jesus, I yearn for Your chastity to reign in me!
O Holy Spirit, I submit all my desires to You!

Day 13 – A Story of Virtuous Cleanliness of Heart

Language. Yes, we all hear it in the hallways or subways. Yes, we are all exposed to it, often innocently, on social media. I wonder about the speakers' upbringing and how they survived just the rough vocabulary, forget about other forms of abuse. I pray that the Holy Spirit cleanses *all of them* — their hearts and souls.

Benjamin was only able to control his language once he started counseling. His mother had left him, and his dad was abusive. His home was a "junkyard," in his words. He chose to live with his grandmother at fifteen to save himself. Using crass language was the norm until the counselor gave him the freedom to express his hurt about his lack of self-worth, stemming from a lack of approval.

What am I saying to my family and friends? Am I able to say, "You are the Father's beloved child. You are worthy, and You are His Jewel. You were bought with His Precious Blood?"

Jesus: "My Child, let Me cleanse your heart, your thoughts, and your words."

I: "Jesus, please clean deeply everything from within me. I cling to Your crucified Body – help me be pure."

Avalanche of Grace!

Day 14 – Virtue of Peace-Making

Today we use the term "peace" in at least seven different ways. Three relate to the individual. Three have to do with society. The seventh pertains to both.

1. Inner Peace

The idea of inner peace speaks of the absence of internal conflicts. "Are you at peace about your decision?" we might ask a friend. This type of peace can reflect psychological health for a person with a well-formed conscience, or conversely, serious problems for the person who is "at peace" with doing something that is morally depraved. The latter is a false peace—the type of delusion that the prophet Jeremiah denounced when he wrote, "'Peace, peace!' they say, though there is no peace" (Jer. 6:14; 8:11).

2. Peace in the Community

The individual is at peace with his family, friends, and neighbors. Harmony with those whom we love and live with is vital to human flourishing and happiness. It also takes much hard work. The Scriptures praise friendship as an essential part of a full life: "A faithful friend is a sturdy shelter; he who finds one finds a treasure. A faithful friend is beyond price, no sum can balance his worth. A faithful friend is a lifesaving remedy, such as he who fears God finds; for he that fears God behaves accordingly, and his friend will be like himself" (Sir. 6:14-17).

3. Peace with God

By the grace of God, a person is placed into right relationship with him. God freely gives this peace of soul. Jesus spoke of this peace to his disciples: "Peace I leave with you, my own peace I give to you; a peace the world cannot give, this is my gift to you. Let not your hearts be troubled or afraid..." (John 14:27). Because this peace is God's gift of reconciliation that he offers to all, we need only accept his offer of friendship.

4. Civil Order

A community is said to be at peace if it is not engaged in civil war or unrest, strife or rebellion. Some disharmony will always exist in any society. We speak of wars against crime and drugs, poverty and disease. But in an obvious way, Costa Rica's civil society is at peace while Somalia's and Sudan's are not.

5. Absence of War

Any society that is not actively engaged in military action can be said to be at peace. Nonetheless, history and the present day offer us plenty of examples where this use of the term falls well short of what one would hope. The German occupation of France and the Japanese conquest of the Philippines in World War II created a "peace" of sorts, but use of the word in this context would be a very limited understanding of the fullness of peace between nations.

6. Tranquility of Order

St. Augustine's classic *The City of God* gives us a more complete way of talking about peace between people and nation-states. Augustine writes that "peace is the calm that comes from order" (XIX:13). In Latin this reads, in part, *pax omnium rerum tranquillitas ordinis* (Peace is a result of a tranquility of order). Twenty years ago, George Weigel defined *tranquillitas ordinis* as "the peace of public order in a dynamic political community" (*Tranquillitas Ordinis: The Present Failure and Future Promise of American Catholic Thought on War and Peace*, 31). The most complete way of discussing peace between nations is to talk of the goal of a dynamic order that is based upon justice and respect for human rights.

7. Eschatological Peace

Finally, peace will come at the end of time, when Christ establishes once and for all the Kingdom. This is the eschatological peace of the end times when all things will be renewed in Christ and "every knee will bow… and every tongue confess to the glory of God the Father that Jesus Christ is Lord" (Phil. 2:10-11). This will be peace in the complete sense, *shalôm* in its fullness. It is the peace described by the prophet Isaiah when he says that we "shall beat our swords into plowshares and our spears into pruning hooks; one nation shall not raise the sword against another, nor shall they train for war again" (Is. 2:4). At the end time, in the fullness of the Kingdom, the lion will lie with the lamb and the child play at the cobra's den (cf. Is. 11).

(Excerpt from Msgr. Stuart Swetland's, "A Primer on Peace.")

Avalanche of Grace!

Day 14 – Reflections on the Virtue of Peace-Making

"Blessed are the peacemakers for they shall be called children of God" — Matthew 5:9.

"Be at peace with your own soul. Then, heaven and earth will be at peace with you" — St. Jerome.

"Acquire the spirit of peace and thousands around you will be saved" — St. Seraphim of Sarov.

"Oh, sons of Peace, sons of the One Catholic, walk in your way, and sing in your walk. Travelers do this in order to keep up their spirits" — St. Augustine of Hippo.

"What can you do to promote world peace? Go home and love your family" — St. Teresa of Calcutta.

"Walk very simply with the Cross of Christ and be at peace with yourself" — St. Francis de Sales.

"Never be in a hurry; do everything quietly and with a calm spirit. Do not lose your inner peace for anything whatsoever, even if your whole world seems upset" — St. Francis de Sales.

Avalanche of Grace!

Day 14 – Prayer for the Virtue of Peace-Making

Read God's Word: John 14: 1-31

O Father, Everlasting Father!
O Jesus, Prince of Peace!
O Holy Spirit, Spirit of Self-Control!

Come Holy Spirit and fill me with Your peace!
I ask for inner peace in all my choices and decisions.
I ask for harmony in my family and community.
I ask for God's peace via His gift of reconciliation.
I ask for civil order in my state, nation, and world.
I ask for the presence of peace and absence of war.
I ask for justice and respect to flow from order.
I ask for Kingdom peace for all souls at the end of time.

Lord, may Your spirit of peace calm every storm!

O Father, as Your child, I wish to work for peace!
O Jesus, Your reign of peace is forever, eternally!
O Holy Spirit, root out seeds of discord on earth!

Day 14 – A Story of Virtuous Peace-Making

Faye knew in her heart that it is God who gives life and He who takes it away. But, the voices of her boyfriend's and her mother's potential wrath in finding out drowned God's voice in her spirit.

Faye's boyfriend took her to the clinic to have their baby aborted at eight weeks. She cried for days after and her depression led her boyfriend to leave her at what would have been the tenth week of her baby's life.

A year later, Faye restored her relationship with God and found peace through the Sacrament of Reconciliation at a women's conference. Eight years later, Faye, happily married with three kids, found herself carrying a fourth. Confronted by anti-big family meddlers, she prayed, "Our Lady of Guadalupe, cover this child with your mantle. I consecrate her/him to Jesus through Your Immaculate Heart, Mary." Faye successfully gave birth to her fourth child, Andrew, for the Prince of Peace reigned in her soul.

Jesus: "My Child, let Me bring you peace. I place a drop of My healing blood upon your heart when you come to confession."

I: "Jesus, I plead Your forgiveness. Restore my broken heart caused by my sin. Use me to be a peace-maker."

Avalanche of Grace!

Day 15 – *Virtue of Resilience*

Many of the world's religions and ancient philosophies extol the benefits of solitude, silence and mindfulness. But their value has only recently gained traction in our world, and then only for its purely psychological worth. …

Solitude and silence allow us to take a step back from societal and cultural forces and really get back to basics. If I don't take some time each day, I find myself lost and confused. …

That time is essential. During the day I can tap back into it, fall back into that solitude moment. It's not a chore or a duty. It's my contemplative period, my time to center and breathe.

Fr. Henri Nouwen said that solitude is not being alone with yourself, but being alone with God; silence is not listening to yourself but to God. Silence intensifies [your interaction with God], and solitude makes the silence richer and deeper.

Mindfulness is key, too. It is really amazing how much we fail to be present to the things around us. Mindfulness, when it's formal, is meditation; informal mindfulness is just being present to the people and events around us. Mindfulness can be learned.

Another way to increased resiliency is facing failure in a productive way. I've often told the groups of people in the helping professions I work with that they should fail more than any other group. With failure, you're able to reassess how you're doing, gaining a natural sense of humility. Knowledge plus humility equals wisdom. Add wisdom to compassion and you get love. Failure is a deepening factor that allows us to put things in perspective and move away from the savior complex.

Another path to increased resiliency is recognizing your own resistance to change. When I work with patients in psychotherapy I try to get them to be intrigued by their resistance to growth and change.

Make friends with resistance. The defenses you put up to resist change are exaggerations of your gifts. In those areas where we feel most vulnerable is where the most resistance often is. If you can become intrigued by it, then it becomes an exploration into your own inner self and what you can do. Under-standing resilience and practicing exercises that lead to self knowledge and mindfulness can deepen our resources and make a difference in the world.

(Excerpts of Robert J. Wicks' *Bounce: Living the Resilient Life* as reprinted in Rick Heffern's "Make a Difference in the World by Being Resilient," *National Catholic Register*).

Day 15 – Reflections on the Virtue of Resilience

"Blessed are they who are persecuted for the sake of righteousness, for theirs is the kingdom of heaven. Blessed are you when they insult you and persecute you and utter every kind of evil against you [falsely] because of me"
—Matthew 5: 10-11.

"I am the wheat of God. Let me be ground by the teeth of wild beasts, that I may be found the pure bread of Christ"
—St. Ignatius of Antioch.

"I fear nothing for God is with me" —St. Joan of Arc.

"One cannot desire freedom from the Cross, when one is especially chosen for the Cross" —St. Edith Stein.

"You wouldn't abandon ship in a storm because you could not control the winds" —St. Thomas More.

"The martyrs gave their blood for the truth, and you are not able to come to Church? They gave their lives for Christ and you are not able to make a small journey for Him? But you say, 'I am a sinner, I cannot come.' Then come and cease to be one!"
—St. John Chrysostom.

Avalanche of Grace!

Day 15 – Prayer for the Virtue of Resilience

Read God's Word: 2 Corinthians 4: 7-18

O Father, Resilient Father, who desires the good of all!
O Jesus, Crucified Son of God and Son of Man!
O Holy Spirit, Comforter of the Persecuted!

I wish to grow in the virtue of resilience that I may:
be ground wheat to become the pure Body of Christ;
be crushed grapes to become the Most Precious Blood;
fear nothing, knowing that God is with and in me;
embrace all insults and pain as I am chosen in You;
stay in the eye of the storm in rough winds;
and, let my blood be spilled in defending the truth.

Teach me, Lord, to choose You every second!
You died for me; help me offer my life for You.

O Father, You patiently create new souls for Yourself!
O Jesus, Your Mercy is the fruit of Your Suffering!
O Holy Spirit, I ask for Your grace to die a witness!

Day 15 – A Story of Virtuous Resilience

At the heart of the gift of resilience is looking out for the good of the other in friendship and Christian charity. Children, for the most part, are said to be very resilient. Teens have great capability for growing in that virtue. Such is Liam's story. My sister, Susan, had given her teenage son, Liam, two ten dollar notes for food and other expenses of the day.

Liam happened to be in Koreatown when he saw a homeless guy who was hungry. Liam gave him a ten dollar bill for food. As he walked away from the poor man, the latter cried aloud, "For another ten, I will be able to get some shelter and bed tonight."

Liam went back to him and gave him the remaining ten dollar note – all that he had. When he got back from school that day, he said to his mother, "I am hungry, mom."

Becoming a white or red martyr for Christ is the crowning act of many little acts of charity; hunger trains the soul for laying down one's life.

Jesus: "My Child, I want all your thoughts, words, and deeds to be offered for Me, in your witness to others."

I: "Jesus, little by little, I want to offer it all for You."

Avalanche of Grace!

Day 16 – Virtue of Contrition

...[It] may be said that there are two conversions: the conversion from sin to self and the conversion from self to God. In the first stage, the thought of God is indeed present, but the sense of one's own misery and loss is the strongest. In the second, the thought of self has almost disappeared; the soul is glad to suffer, complains of nothing, rejoices if by all it has to endure it can make reparation to the love of God, against which it has sinned.

Contrition, then, in a more or less perfect form, is to be found at the very beginning of the spiritual life of all those who have ever sinned deeply. It is its first movement, that which causes it to say, "I will arise." It is the first thought that breaks in upon the soul as it awakens to the sense of its sin. "When he came to himself he said, "How many hired servants of my Father have bread enough to spare, and I perish with hunger. I will arise and go to my Father!"...

...[W]hen old temptations come back with redoubled force, when the power of habit reasserts itself, when all the succors of grace seem to be withdrawn and the soul is left face-to-face with the multitude of her enemies, conscious only that the will has no strength to resist [then] it is that contrition comes to the rescue, and her power is felt as never before. Her power — and yet she herself seems so weak — for the inspiration of love seems to have died out of her too; yet still she is there in the thick of the fight, standing by the will, urging it on with arguments, appealing to it, strengthening it; and when every fortress of the soul seems overthrown, contrition holds the will and gains the victory…

…Its transforming power is so great that it can fit the greatest sinner for the company of the saints. The Magdalene was not out of place by the side of the spotless Mother. …

Contrition Is Patient

Contrition is ready to endure all that comes upon it, whether justly or unjustly; it knows what it deserves, and it knows that if others knew it as it truly is, it could be treated with no consideration or kindness. It recognizes that it has no rights; that the chief reason that it is permitted to live is in order that reparation may, in some degree, be done for the past. It bears about within itself an awakened conscience that speaks as the representative of the justice of the all-holy God; and the voice of conscience is ever passing sentence upon it, and the soul, in the spirit of penitence, is ever more and more ready to welcome everything as acting toward it for the satisfaction of an offended God. Nay, it longs to find new offerings to make, for it can never lose sight of God's love, and it knows that whatever it may have to suffer is not a mere penalty sent in anger, but a loving chastisement to restore and perfect it.

...And it accepts above all things the consequences of past sin without a murmur, the constant presence of temptation, the sense of weakness and of loss, the deadness of heart, the poverty of prayer, the very fear of self-deception, the agony of doubt that at times darkens all the path, filling it with uncertainty, whether its penitence is real or whether, after all, it is not a specious form of self-interest...

...And what if the power of old sin asserts itself and it yields again and falls? Even then it does not lose patience or despair but, with a deeper sense of need, strives to cling more closely to God. ...

Contrition Is Strong

Contrition shows its strength by what it puts away rather than by what it does. It puts away those things with which it has formerly sinned. If by necessity it has them as part of its life, it puts them away from the heart.

That which has been an occasion of sin must be a memorial of sorrow. We may be violent in active antagonism to sin while we are continually recurring to objects that have been the causes of sin; but contrition puts them away, and at whatever cost. We may hate sin very much and yet feel that we must have certain things, indulgences, and friendships that have been the cause of sin in the past...

Contrition Is Tender

Contrition has no harshness. It springs from the love of God. It does not come before the mind as a duty; it springs out of the heart by the necessity of its own inspiration. It is the longing of a soul burdened with the sense of defilement to be conformed to the holiness of Him whom it loves. It springs from the love of God, not from the hatred of sin. ...

...[T]here is none [that is, the asceticism of the Christian penitent] so tender toward others, so sensitive for their well-being, so slow to condemn or to see others' faults. It seems to it as if all the world needs kindness and care except itself. Contrition closes the eyes toward the sins of others and opens them upon its own; it sees itself as the one culprit in the midst of a world that throbs with the love of God.

(Various excerpts from a chapter in Fr. Basil W. Maturin's book *Spiritual Guidelines for Souls Seeking God* as reflected in *Catholic Exchange's* article "Nurture Genuine Sorrow for Your Sins.")

Avalanche of Grace!

Day 16 – Reflections on the Virtue of Contrition

"But the tax collector stood off at a distance and would not even raise his eyes to heaven but beat his breast and prayed, 'O God, be merciful to me a sinner" —Luke 18:13.

"It is so hard to admit that one is a sinner; it is so hard to climb the hill of Calvary and kneel beneath a cross and ask for pardon, for forgiveness. Certainly it is hard. But it is harder to hang there" —Blessed Fulton Sheen.

"Turn away Your face from my sins; blot out all my iniquities. A clean heart create for me, God; renew within me a steadfast spirit" —Psalm 51: 11-12.

"It is a spiritual gift from God for man to perceive his own sins" —St. Isaac the Syrian.

"Confession is the soul's bath. Even a clean and unoccupied room gathers dust; return after a week and you will see it needs dusting again" —St. Pio of Pietrelcina.

"A single sunbeam is enough to drive away many shadows" —St. Francis of Assisi.

"The sacrifice most pleasing to God is the contrition of heart" —St. Eulogius of Cordova.

Avalanche of Grace!

Day 16 – Prayer for the Virtue of Contrition

Read God's Word: Luke 15:1-32

O Father of Mercy, have compassion on me!
O Jesus, Son of God, have pity on me, a poor sinner!
O Holy Spirit, I ask Your grace for true contrition!

Stir me and move in me to say, "I will arise"
when the wounds of hurtful past relationships surface.
I say, "Lord, Jesus Christ, Son of the Living God, have mercy on me a poor sinner":
for blindness to my own sin and its roots;
for a lack of forgiveness of self, others, and God;
for seeking pleasure in the world and its goods;
for picking at the scabs of past wounds;
Bathe, wash, and cleanse me Holy Trinity!
I make a resolution to return to You – for healing.

O Father, Your mercy is eternal. "I will arise!"
O Jesus, I hear you say, "Go and sin no more!"
O Holy Spirit, may I live a life of true contrition!

Day 16 – A Story of Virtuous Contrition

Dave knew that his own problems stemmed from his mother's alcoholic issues. With mom in rehabilitation, at two and a half years old, Dave was put in foster care. He could not utter a word.

One day, his foster mom prayed a prayer of forgiveness for him and that the Holy Spirit would release his tongue for speech. That night, Dave babbled in the Spirit even as he lied down to sleep. He started speaking whole phrases within days.

Years later, in his late thirties, Dave allowed Jesus to enter His brokenness even in his mother's womb and his first years. Jesus embraced him, nourished him, listened to his needs, talked to him, and played with him.

Dave with a moment of authentic contrition prayed aloud, "In Jesus' Name, I forgive my mom for restraining me in a car seat, for neglecting to feed me, for not carrying me and playing with me, and for abandoning me." This began a new chapter in Dave's life.

Jesus: "My Child, I was there pressing you close to My Heart. I listened and carried you near to my breast."

I: "Jesus, I am truly sorry for abandoning You, and others who needed me most."

Avalanche of Grace!

Day 17 – Virtue of Repentance

SORROW for sin has two aspects, two slants as it were, one backwards and one forward. Looking back, the penitent regrets and detests sin; looking forward, he determines to avoid it.

Determination to avoid both sin and its occasions, in other words, firm purpose of amendment, is the crucial test of the reality of contrition. He who is determined to do his best to avoid sin, undoubtedly has true repentance, even though he feels spiritually dry as a desert and indevout as an iceberg.

The proof of contrition is in the effective will to reform. It is all-important that there should be no misunderstanding about the true meaning of contrition; remorse must on no account be confused with repentance.

Judas said: *"Peccavi"* —- "I have sinned"; David said the same. Judas had remorse; David had repentance. David was contrite, Judas was not. Both were sad about sin, both regretted it, both did not have repentance. Judas made a public confession of sin: "I have sinned in betraying innocent blood"; yet, despite his remorse and confession and restitution of his foully-gotten gains, he did not have effective repentance.

Remorse is a product of wishful-thinking and implies the wish to avoid sin; repentance implies the determined will to avoid it. Remorse is conditional; repentance is absolute.

The remorseful would like to avoid sin if doing so did not entail so much effort and sacrifice, and if he had enough faith, hope and charity. Contrition admits neither "ifs" nor "buts," and does not recognize the sacrosanctity of ruts. The remorseful would like to undo his sin, but he has not the requisite determination to remove the occasions of sin .... .

A well-known principle of scholasticism: *"qui vult finem, vult media"* —- "he who wills the end, wills the means," suggests the only true practical test of contrition, which is —- willingness to use all the necessary means to avoid sin.

If we truly hate sin, we shall do all in our power to avoid it. If, however, we are unwilling to use the means, we deceive ourselves if we fancy that we will the end. Pilate wished to release our Divine Savior; had he willed it, he could have released Him at once.

We must be careful not to confuse velleity and volition. A firm purpose of amendment implies more than a wish or desire; it implies determination.

The firm purpose of amendment is the most difficult act of the penitent. .... St. Alphonsus says that most bad confessions are bad through lack of practical amendment; ...(Excerpts in "Remorse and Repentance" from Alfred Wilson, CP, *Pardon and Peace*).

Day 17 – Reflections on the Virtue of Repentance

"[Zacchaeus said to Jesus], 'Behold, half of my possessions, Lord, I shall give to the poor, and if I have extorted anything from anyone I shall repay it four times over'" — Luke 19: 8.

"... Repent, and believe in the Gospel"— Mark 1: 15.

"God does not judge Christians because they sinned, but because they do not repent" — St. Niphon of Constantia.

"Sin is followed by shame. Repentance is followed by boldness" — St. John Chrysostom.

"Sorrow for sin is indeed necessary, but it should not be an endless preoccupation. You must dwell also on the glad remembrance of God's loving kindness; otherwise, sadness will harden the heart and lead it more deeply into despair"
— St. Bernard Clairvaux.

"Suffering is a great grace; through suffering the soul becomes like the Savior; in suffering love becomes crystallized; the greater the suffering, the purer the love" — St. Faustina Kowalska.

"Woe to me if I prove myself a half-hearted soldier in the service of my thorn-crowned captain"
— St. Fidelis of Sigmaringen.

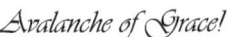

Day 17 – Prayer for the Virtue of Repentance

Read God's Word: 2 Corinthians 6 and 7

O Father, Father, repairer of the breach in souls!
O Jesus, Blood of the Lamb, who saves all souls!
O Holy Spirit, who convicts us for reparation!

Holy Trinity, I no longer wish, but rather *I will* these:
I am the Father's child and desire to live like His child;
in the cross, I want to console Your Heart, Jesus;
in the cross, I make amends for others' and my sin;
in the cross, I offer rosaries and Masses for souls;
in His Presence, I make reparation for indifference;
in His gaze on me, I claim victory over suffering;
in His Divine Praises, I adore His Holy Name;
in His mercy, I become Christ in deeds and words;
and, in His grace, I bear witness of Jesus to all.

O Father, who sent Jesus to take away all sin!
O Jesus, Perfect Sacrifice for all sin and guilt!
O Holy Spirit, help me fill in the lack caused by sin!

Day 17 – A Story of Virtuous Repentance

Will and Anne, Christian evangelists, had two beautiful daughters and a son, when Anne was found with a fourth child. Barely making ends meet as it was, they decided to get a cheap abortion.

As they walked out of the clinic, Will heard the phrase by a bunch with rosary beads, "Hail Mary, full of grace…" The words grated on Will's ears. He shouted, "Why can't you Catholics get it right? Mary is not the fullness of grace. Jesus is." Xavier responded, "Brother, does not scripture say that the angel Gabriel called Mary, 'full of grace?' For Jesus to be grace, God's method of intervention had to be a pure vessel that is filled with grace. Mary, Full of Grace, begets Grace, Jesus. Grace flows from Fullness of Grace. Ask Mary to pour out God's grace on you and your child."

The gravity of the abortion began to sink in. "What have we done?" Anne said. Xavier comforted them with these words, "Take Mary, the Mother of Jesus, home with you. Love all children — see Jesus Himself in them." Will and Anne went and did just that. They joined the Catholics at the fence the next day and many years hence.

Jesus: *"My child, I suffer most in the voiceless unborn."*

I: *"How I wish to console Your Heart in innocent babies."*

Avalanche of Grace!

Day 18 – Virtue of Reparation

The seventh commandment forbids theft. Theft is the usurpation of another's goods against the reasonable will of the owner. Every manner of taking and using another's property unjustly is contrary to the seventh commandment. The injustice committed requires reparation. Commutative justice requires the restitution of stolen goods.

[The eight commandment] "You shall not bear false witness against your neighbor"(*Ex* 20:16). Christ's disciples have "put on the new man, created after the likeness of God in true righteousness and holiness" (*Eph* 4:24). Truth or truthfulness is the virtue which consists in showing oneself true in deeds and truthful in words, and guarding against duplicity, dissimulation, and hypocrisy. The Christian is not to "be ashamed of testifying to our Lord" (2 *Tim* 1:8) in deed and word. Martyrdom is the supreme witness given to the truth of the faith.

Respect for the reputation and honor of persons forbids all detraction and calumny in word or attitude. An offense committed against the truth requires reparation. The golden rule helps one discern, in concrete situations, whether or not it would be appropriate to reveal the truth to someone who asks for it.

(Catechism of the Catholic Church 2453-2454, 2504-2510)

Day 18 – Reflections on the Virtue of Reparation

"My children, —I am writing this to you so that you may not commit sin. But if anyone does sin, we have an Advocate with the Father, Jesus Christ the righteous one. He is expiation for our sins, and not for our sins only but for those of the whole world" —1 John 2:1-2.

"Most Holy Trinity, Father, Son and Holy Spirit, I adore Thee profoundly. I offer Thee the most precious Body, Blood, Soul and Divinity of Jesus Christ, present in all the tabernacles of the world, in reparation for the outrages, sacrileges, and indifference by which He is offended. And through the infinite merits of His Most Sacred Heart, and the Immaculate Heart of Mary, I beg for the conversion of poor sinners"
—Angel at Fatima.

"Trials and tribulations offer us a chance to make reparation for our past faults and sins. On such occasions the Lord comes to us like a physician to heal the wounds left by our sins. Tribulation is the divine medicine" —St. Augustine.

"He who suffers wrong and does not demand reparation from the person who wronged him, trusts in Christ to make good the loss; and he is rewarded a hundredfold in this world and inherits life" —St. Mark the Ascetic.

Avalanche of Grace!

Day 18 – Prayer for the Virtue of Reparation

Read God's Word: Colossians 1: 1-29

O Father, Father Forever, I ask for Your mercy!
O Jesus, I trust in Your Divine Mercy always!
O Holy Spirit, I ask for more desire for reparation!

O Holy Trinity, I wish to make reparation for:
taking from You and Yours – reverence and awe;
stealing from others – their goods and reputation;
others' faults, failings, and sins, from past to present;
a lack of true renewal in my thoughts, acts, and deeds;
offenses against You in the Blessed Sacrament;
sacrileges and indifference to Your Divine Sacrifice;
my lack of humble prayers for the souls in purgatory;
and, all my imperfect past sacrifices and mortifications.

O Jesus, repair my poor soul in Your Holy Soul.

O Father, Father Forever, forgive me all my sins!
O Jesus, Atonement, completely satisfied, save me!
O Holy Spirit, I ask to fill what lacks in the Body!

Day 18 – A Story of Virtuous Reparation

1981. The Indian Airlines pilot dropped one of his engines and prepared the passengers for a crash landing. *All* got into a fetal position.

With his rosary in hand, Georgie prayed, "Please, Lord, take care of Kitty and the children." Georgie was heading back home from a business trip to Belgium, a London trip to visit my brother Godwin (who cut his long hair and quit smoking after dad left), and a pilgrimage to Lourdes to thank Our Blessed Mother for saving Georgie himself from colon cancer eight years prior.

After the pilot belly-landed the plane on a field, stopping just a hundred feet short of a retaining wall, smoke filled the cabin. Georgie shouted to the passengers, "Forget your duty-free wine! Forget your belongings! Get out of the plane!" Then, he helped women and children to safety. Not one life was lost.

Georgie's once rectangular suitcase arrived a month later, looking like a chocolate bow-tie. Amma opened the bag to find his clothes intact and as fresh as new. "Our Lady of Lourdes' blessed water spilt and kept my garments from stain and smell," Georgie said.

Jesus: "My child, your thankfulness repairs My soul."

I: "Jesus, I want to 'awe' you forever as reparation."

Avalanche of Grace!

Day 19 – Virtue of Balanced Passions

The term "passions" belongs to the Christian patrimony. Feelings or passions are emotions or movements of the sensitive appetite that incline us to act or not to act in regard to something felt or imagined to be good or evil.

The passions are natural components of the human psyche; the passageway and ensure the connection between the life of the senses and the life of the mind. Our Lord called man's heart the source from which the passions spring.[40]

There are many passions. The most fundamental passion is love, aroused by the attraction of the good. Love causes a desire for the absent good and the hope of obtaining it; this movement finds completion in the pleasure and joy of the good possessed. The apprehension of evil causes hatred, aversion, and fear of the impending evil; this movement ends in sadness at some present evil, or in the anger that resists it.

"To love is to will the good of another."[41] All other affections have their source in this first movement of the human heart toward the good. Only the good can be loved.[42] Passions "are evil if love is evil and good if it is good."[43]

In themselves passions are neither good nor evil. They are morally qualified only to the extent that they effectively engage reason and will. Passions are said to be voluntary, "either because they are commanded by the will or because the will does not place obstacles in their way."[44] It belongs to the perfection of the moral or human good that the passions be governed by reason.[45]

Strong feelings are not decisive for the morality or the holiness of persons; they are simply the inexhaustible reservoir of images and affections in which the moral life is expressed. Passions are morally good when they contribute to a good action, evil in the opposite case. The upright will orders the movements of the senses it appropriates to the good and to beatitude; an evil will succumbs to disordered passions and exacerbates them. Emotions and feelings can be taken up into the virtues or perverted by the *vices*.

In the Christian life, the Holy Spirit himself accomplishes his work by mobilizing the whole being, with all its sorrows, fears and sadness, as is visible in the Lord's agony and passion. In Christ human feelings are able to reach their consummation in charity and divine beatitude.

Moral perfection consists in man's being moved to the good not by his will alone, but also by his sensitive appetite, as in the words of the psalm: "My heart and flesh sing for joy to the living God."[46]

(Catechism of the Catholic Church 1762-1775)

Day 19 – Reflections on the Virtue of Balanced Passions

"Now those who belong to Christ [Jesus] have crucified their flesh with its passions and desires. If we live in the Spirit, let us also follow the Spirit. Let us not be conceited, provoking one another, envious of one another" —Galatians 5:24.

"It is better to cry than be angry because anger hurts others while tears flow silently through the soul and cleanse the heart" —St. John Paul II.

"The passion of Jesus is a sea of sorrows but it is also an ocean of love. Ask the Lord to teach you to fish in this ocean. Dive into its depths. No matter how deep you go, you will never reach the bottom" —St. Paul of the Cross.

"To yield and give way to our passions is the lowest slavery, even as to rule over them is the only liberty" —St. Justin Martyr.

"Fasting cleanses the soul, raises the mind, subjects one's flesh to the spirit, renders the heart contrite and humble, scatters the clouds of concupiscence, quenches the fires of lust, and kindles the true light of chastity" —St. Augustine.

"There is nothing we can desire or want that we do not find in God" —St. Catherine of Siena.

Avalanche of Grace!

Day 19 – Prayer for the Virtue of Balanced Passions

Read God's Word: 2 Peter 1: 1-21

O Father, I want to desire You above all!
O Jesus, I want Your passion to flow in my heart!
O Holy Spirit, I ask to be filled with love for all!

Father, empty my reservoir of desire for creatures
and things. Fill me with Your holy waters of love!
Jesus, help me love like You by willing the good
of the other! Fill my heart with Your pure intentions!
Holy Spirit, direct all my senses to beatitude.
Fill me with a sweet passion for Jesus, and a firm
commitment to not allow gossip, lust, anger, jealousy,
or pride, to get in the way of my loving others.

Holy Trinity, in Your tripod of love, balance
my desires, emotions, and passions with holy reason.

O Father, You desire my heart! I desire Yours!
O Jesus, I unite my feelings to Your divine Charity!
O Holy Spirit, I submit all my passions to You!

Avalanche of Grace!

Day 19 – A Story of Virtuous Balanced Passions

A daughter of wisdom and a sensitive soul, Dina sensed gossip behind her back. She knew when the jealous person was present. She sensed the fiery darts of anger in the eyes of her sister, Noelle, who resisted the Holy Spirit's gentle call to God's ways.

Yes, Dina spent time listening to Jesus. She had "chosen the better part." But, she also went all out to pray about her own interactions with her Noelle.

Dina prayed to the Lord humbly and lovingly:

> Jesus, You know that I am at Your feet because I truly cannot *do* as much as Noelle. So Noelle is partly right. Here I am taking delight in You, instead of doing my share. Give me the grace to call out Noelle's talents of service that I may see again in her eyes, the light of Your eyes! Give me the grace to help dissipate her anger by giving her some time off to contemplate You. Give me the physical strength to offer to do the meals, the cleaning and the washing from time to time. Amen.

Jesus: "My child, help those around you to choose Me. I wish to be loved with the passion of Mary."

I: "Jesus, I ask for the gift of ordering the passions within and without me that give rise to jealousy, anger, and conflict."

Avalanche of Grace!

Day 20 – Virtue of a Moral Conscience

Deep within his conscience man discovers a law which he has not laid upon himself but which he must obey. Its voice, ever calling him to love and to do what is good and to avoid evil, sounds in his heart at the right moment. . . . For man has in his heart a law inscribed by God. . . . His conscience is man's most secret core and his sanctuary. There he is alone with God whose voice echoes in his depths.[47]

I. THE JUDGMENT OF CONSCIENCE

Moral conscience,[48] present at the heart of the person, enjoins him at the appropriate moment to do good and to avoid evil. It also judges particular choices, approving those that are good and denouncing those that are evil.[49] It bears witness to the authority of truth in reference to the supreme Good to which the human person is drawn, and it welcomes the commandments. When he listens to his conscience, the prudent man can hear God speaking.

Conscience is a judgment of reason whereby the human person recognizes the moral quality of a concrete act that he is going to perform, is in the process of performing, or has already completed. In all he says and does, man is obliged to follow faithfully what he knows to be just and right. It is by the judgment of his conscience that man perceives and recognizes the prescriptions of the divine law:

> Conscience is a law of the mind; yet [Christians] would not grant that it is nothing more; I mean that it was not a dictate, nor conveyed the notion of responsibility, of duty, of a threat and a promise. ... [Conscience] is a messenger of him, who, both in nature and in grace, speaks to us behind a veil, and teaches and rules us by his representatives. Conscience is the aboriginal Vicar of Christ.[50]

It is important for every person to be sufficiently present to himself in order to hear and follow the voice of his conscience. This requirement of *interiority* is all the more necessary as life often distracts us from any reflection, self-examination or introspection:

> Return to your conscience, question it. ... Turn inward, brethren, and in everything you do, see God as your witness.[51]

The dignity of the human person implies and requires *uprightness of moral conscience*. Conscience includes the perception of the principles of morality (synderesis); their application in the given circumstances by practical discernment of reasons and goods; and finally judgment about concrete acts yet to be performed or already performed. The truth about the moral good, stated in the law of reason, is recognized practically and concretely by the *prudent judgment* of conscience. We call that man prudent who chooses in conformity with this judgment.

Conscience enables one to assume *responsibility* for the acts performed. If man commits evil, the just judgment of conscience can remain within him as the witness to the universal truth of the good, at the same time as the evil of his particular choice. The verdict of the judgment of conscience remains a pledge of hope and mercy. In attesting to the fault committed, it calls to mind the forgiveness that must be asked, the good that must still be practiced, and the virtue that must be constantly cultivated with the grace of God:

> We shall . . . reassure our hearts before him whenever our hearts condemn us; for God is greater than our hearts, and he knows everything.[52]

Man has the right to act in conscience and in freedom so as personally to make moral decisions. "He must not be forced to act contrary to his conscience. Nor must he be prevented from acting according to his conscience, especially in religious matters."[53]

II. THE FORMATION OF CONSCIENCE

Conscience must be informed and moral judgment enlightened. A well-formed conscience is upright and truthful. It formulates its judgments according to reason, in conformity with the true good willed by the wisdom of the Creator. The education of conscience is indispensable for human beings who are subjected to negative influences and tempted by sin to prefer their own judgment and to reject authoritative teachings.

The education of the conscience is a lifelong task. From the earliest years, it awakens the child to the knowledge and practice of the interior law recognized by conscience. Prudent education teaches virtue; it prevents or cures fear, selfishness and pride, resentment arising from guilt, and feelings of complacency, born of human weakness and faults. The education of the conscience guarantees freedom and engenders peace of heart.

In the formation of conscience the Word of God is the light for our path,[54] we must assimilate it in faith and prayer and put it into practice. We must also examine our conscience before the Lord's Cross. We are assisted by the gifts of the Holy Spirit, aided by the witness or advice of others and guided by the authoritative teaching of the Church.[55]

III. TO CHOOSE IN ACCORD WITH CONSCIENCE

Faced with a moral choice, conscience can make either a right judgment in accordance with reason and the divine law or, on the contrary, an erroneous judgment that departs from them.

Man is sometimes confronted by situations that make moral judgments less assured and decision difficult.

But he must always seriously seek what is right and good and discern the will of God expressed in divine law.

To this purpose, man strives to interpret the data of experience and the signs of the times assisted by the virtue of prudence, by the advice of competent people, and by the help of the Holy Spirit and his gifts.

Some rules apply in every case:
- One may never do evil so that good may result from it;
- the Golden Rule: "Whatever you wish that men would do to you, do so to them."[56]
- charity always proceeds by way of respect for one's neighbor and his conscience: "Thus sinning against your brethren and wounding their conscience . . . you sin against Christ."[57] Therefore "it is right not to . . . do anything that makes your brother stumble."[58]

(Catechism of the Catholic Church 1776-1788)

Day 20 – Reflections on the Virtue of a Moral Conscience

"Therefore, brothers, since through the blood of Jesus we have confidence of entrance into the sanctuary— by the new and living way he opened for us through the veil, that is, his flesh, and since we have 'a great priest over the house of God,' let us approach with a sincere heart and in absolute trust, with our hearts sprinkled clean from an evil conscience – and our bodies washed in pure water"— Hebrews 10:19-22.

"Conscience is the aboriginal Vicar of Christ"
—St. John Henry Newman.

"Moral principles do not depend on a majority vote. Wrong is wrong even if everybody is wrong. Right is right, even if nobody is right"—Blessed Fulton Sheen.

"There are two victims in every abortion: a dead baby and a dead conscience"—St. Teresa of Calcutta.

"I do not care very much what men say of me, provided that God approves of me"—St. Thomas More.

"I am not afraid. I was born to do this"—St. Joan of Arc.

"Those who remain silent are responsible"—St. Edith Stein.

Avalanche of Grace!

Day 20 – Prayer for the Virtue of A Moral Conscience

Read God's Word: Acts 23: 1-35

O Father, Supreme author of all conscience!
O Jesus, by grace's Veil, You instruct my soul!
O Holy Spirit, I ask to listen to God's voice!

O Holy Trinity, I offer my conscience to You to:
do good and avoid evil at all times;
use holy judgment in choices set before me;
bear witness to Your truth and reject lies;
act according to the Catholic faith in all things;
mold my conscience to become free;
and, be endowed with a lasting grace of interiority.

O Christ, You are the soul of my conscience.
O Christ, One of Your thorns, I ask, to live in truth!
O Christ, I live free in Your thoughts and ways!

O Father, You are the finisher of my conscience!
O Jesus, let love be the crowning jewel in my soul!
O Holy Spirit, I ask for the grace to follow God!

Avalanche of Grace!

Day 20 – A Story of Virtuous Moral Conscience

Julieta was overwhelmed with taking care of her three kids, ages 7, 5, and 2. Alfonso, the father of her children, was not fully invested in spending time with them. So Julieta looked for diversions, – choosing a healthy one – to get an education.

But Alfonso was now left to take care of the kids while Julieta went to college. He was frustrated with child-care, leaving Julieta with more than she could handle when she got home. So she took to drinking, lying, and cheating on Alfonso. Alfonso, who had a possessive streak in him, had previously threatened to take his life if Julieta ever left him.

Julieta now carried a fourth child, not knowing who the father of the child was. With the kids, she left Alfonso, retreating to her mother's place to find her conscience. Her mother gave her a home not knowing the whole truth.

Julieta, clasping her mother's hands, was able to ask in her heart, "What have I done to you my God? What have I done to my family's soul and my own soul? Forgive me, Lord, for I am a sinner."

Jesus: *"My child, You are my child, no matter your past and present. Will you let me enter into your future?"*

I: *"Jesus, please help me make holy choices for my soul."*

Day 21 – Virtue of Detachment

Detachment from human beings does not mean that we are to love no one on this earth, but it means that our inclinations are to be in accordance with the Will of God and pleasing to Him. Both nature and religion impose upon us the obligation of loving our parents, relatives, and benefactors. But this love becomes inordinate and bad when it leads us to offend God, and impedes our progress in a virtuous life. Many Christians would make great progress on the road to perfection were they freed from all earthly attachments. But because they foster some inordinate attachment in their hearts and are unwilling to renounce it, they continue in their lamentable condition, without advancing a single step on the way of virtue. St. John of the Cross says, "A soul that is attached to any creature will never attain perfect union with God, even though that soul possesses many other virtues." It matters very little whether a bird is bound by a strong or weak cord, for the bird remains a captive and unable to fly as long as the cord is not broken. It is sad to see so many souls who are otherwise rich in virtues and graces, but who never reach a perfect union with God because they have not courage to renounce some little attachment.

Avalanche of Grace!

(Excerpt from the German of Rev. Paul Leick by Rev. Cornelius J. Warren based on St. Alphonsus Liguori's *The 12 Steps to Holiness and Salvation*, 83-84.)

Day 21 – Reflections on the Virtue of Detachment

"I am the good shepherd. A good shepherd lays down his life for his sheep" —John 10:11.

"Love does not consist in feeling great things but having great detachment and in suffering for the Beloved (God)"
—St. John of the Cross.

"Blessed is the man who makes himself deaf to every pleasure that separates him from his Creator" —St. Isaac the Syrian.

"Let us detach ourselves in spirit from all that we see and cling to that which we believe" —St. Peter Damian.

"He who covets possessions will never become a saint"
—St. Philip Neri.

"Live in the world as if God and your soul only were in it; so shall your heart be never made captive by any earthly thing"
—St. John of the Cross.

"I love you because You are the sole object worthy of my love. I love You because You are goodness itself. I love You because You have promised. You have sworn never to abandon me. I love You, O Lord, for an infinity of reasons"
—St. Gemma Galgani.

Avalanche of Grace!

Day 21 – Prayer for the Virtue of Detachment

Read God's Word: Luke 18: 18-30

O Father, I came with nought, with nought I leave!
O Jesus, I renounce all unhealthy cords for You!
O Holy Spirit, I ask Your grace to break such cords!

Holy Trinity, I want to embrace You fully.
No matter if I feel You, I want my faith to be alive.
Release me from attachments to my fears, anxieties, impatience, anger, and depression, *O Sweet Trinity!*
Release me from attachments to comfort, distractions, approval and praise by others, *O Sweet Trinity!*
and, release me from attachments to people, power, control, privilege, and influence, *O Sweet Trinity!*

I desire to knit my soul with Yours, *O Sweet Trinity.*
I offer all of me to You, *O Sweet Trinity.*

O Father, thank You for Your breath of life in me!
O Jesus, thank You for showing me how to let go!
O Holy Spirit, thank You for being my sole desire!

Day 21 – A Story of Virtuous Detachment

Different jobs, different homes, different people, different languages, different cultures, different cities, different countries, and different parish families. God sent Sara to be a witness. As a young person, Sara had said, "Here, I am. Send me!" Sent, she went. She taught. In His Name, the Name above all Names, she let the Holy Spirit bring healing to those whom she evangelized.

Now, as an older person with a young soul, Sara reflected on the time she wished so badly to plant roots but the words that took root in her soul were *"Foxes have dens, and the birds of the air have nests, but the Son of Man has nowhere to rest His head"* (Matt. 8:20).

Sara totally attaches herself to Jesus in the Eucharist. She prays daily, "I desire and want only what You want for me and for all souls, Jesus! Empty each soul completely of all disordered affections and fill them with the power of your Holy Spirit." Sara gears up to go one more time, to one soul at a time.

Jesus: "My child, I take your hand and run with You to spread My Love to a world that is forgetting Me."

I: "Jesus, I offer up everyone to Your heart whom I have been called to witness to in the past, present, and future."

Day 22 – Virtue of Total Abandonment

Abandonment to God is for you just now the one thing necessary. To effect this thoroughly I give you the following rules:

1st. When you go to prayer you must be resigned to suffer at it, to be tormented and exactly as God pleases. When distractions, aridity, temptations, and weariness overwhelm you, say, "You are welcome, Cross of my God; I embrace You with a resigned will; make me suffer until my self-love becomes crucified and dead." Then, remain in God's presence like a beast of burden weighed down with its load, and almost ready to perish, but expecting succor and help from its Master. If you could but throw yourself in spirit at the foot of the cross of Jesus Christ, humbly kiss His sacred wounds, and remain there at His divine feet steadfast and motionless, and do nothing else but wait patiently in silence and peace as a poor beggar waits for hours at a time at the gates of a great king, or of a generous and rich benefactor, hoping to receive an alms. But before all things do not dream of making any more efforts, either in prayer, or in anything else, trying to be more recollected than God wishes you to be…

(Excerpt from Father Jean Pierre de Caussade's *Abandonment to Divine Providence*, 242-243.)

Day 22 – Reflections on the Virtue of Total Abandonment

"...I have been crucified with Christ; yet I live, no longer I, but Christ lives in me; insofar as I now live in the flesh, I live by faith in the Son of God who has loved me and given himself up for me" —Galatians 2: 19-20.

"Abandon yourself into the hands of Mary. She will take care of you" —St. Pio of Pietrelcina.

"Few souls understand what God would accomplish in them if they were to abandon themselves unreservedly to Him and if they were to allow His grace to mold them accordingly" —St. Ignatius of Loyola.

"Abandonment alone brings me into your arms, O Jesus" —St. Therese of Lisieux.

"Even while living in this world, the heart of Mary was so filled with tenderness and compassion for men, that no one ever suffered so much for his own pains as Mary suffered for the pains of others" —St. Jerome.

"Do not abandon yourselves to despair. We are the Easter people and Hallelujah is our song" —St. John Paul II.

"Prefer nothing, absolutely nothing, to the love of Christ" —St. Benedict of Nursia.

Avalanche of Grace!

Day 22 – Prayer for the Virtue of Total Abandonment

Read God's Word: Luke 23: 33-49

O *Abba* Father, I am Your child and only Yours!
O Jesus, I am crucified with You!
O Holy Spirit, I place all my gifts in Your Heart!

Holy Trinity, I abandon myself completely to You.
I surrender all my cares and worries to You –
You take care of me, *Abba*, Jesus, and Sweet Spirit.
I place all my needs and wants into Your Heart –
You are all I need, *Abba*, Jesus, and Holy Spirit.
I give the desires of my heart to You –
You are all I desire, *Abba*, Jesus, and Sweet Spirit.
I possess nothing save You, my true treasure –
take possession of me, *Abba*, Jesus, and Holy Spirit.
I am nothing for I was created by You and for You –
You are my all, *Abba*, Jesus, and Sweet Spirit.

O Father, I run to Your embrace every minute!
O Jesus, I cling to Your Heart! Do not let go of me!
O Holy Spirit, I abandon my heart to Your control!

Day 22 – A Story of Virtuous Total Abandonment

Madison's children approached her, knowing that she had gone through a painful separation from their dad many years before. "Surely, we have room for Dad. He has no medical insurance. He is dying." The proverbial parent who left for another person and had more children now needs to come back. What options did Madison have?

Madison went to the Blessed Mother, "Mother Mary, please tell me what I should do." Mary spoke to the depths of her heart, "Take care of my son."

Madison took her children's father in to care for him. She fed him. She washed him. She talked with him. She prayed with him. She forgave him. Not because he deserved it, but because Jesus and the Blessed Mother wanted that of her. Madison abandoned her will to His Will by binding the wounds of the one who had abandoned her.

Jesus: "My child, total abandonment to Me is like this — You forgive and take care of the souls who have hurt you."

I: "Jesus, I ask for the grace to forgive completely."

Avalanche of Grace!

Day 23 – Virtue of Sacrifice

My daughter, I want to instruct you on how you are to rescue souls through sacrifice and prayer. You will save more souls through prayer and suffering than will a missionary through his teachings and sermons alone. I want to see you as a sacrifice of living love, which only then carries weight before Me. You must be annihilated, destroyed, living as if you were dead in the most secret depths of your being. You must be destroyed in that secret depth where the human eye has never penetrated; then will I find in you a pleasing sacrifice, a holocaust full of sweetness and fragrance. And great will be your power for whomever you intercede. Outwardly, your sacrifice must look like this: silent, hidden, permeated with love, imbued with prayer. I demand, My daughter, that your sacrifice be pure and full of humility, that I may find pleasure in it. I will not spare my grace, that you may be able to fulfill what I demand of you.

I will now instruct you on what your holocaust shall consist of, in everyday life, so as to preserve you from illusions. You shall accept all sufferings with love. Do not be afflicted if your heart often experiences repugnance and dislike for sacrifice. All its power rests in the will, and so these contrary feelings, far from lowering the value of the sacrifice in My eyes, will enhance it. Know that your body and soul will often be in the midst of fire. Although you will not feel My presence on some occasions, I will always be with you. Do not fear; My grace will be with you…

(Excerpt from St. Maria Faustina Kowalska's *Diary: Divine Mercy in My Soul*, Notebook VI, #1767, 627.)

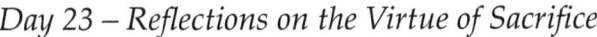
Avalanche of Grace!

Day 23 – Reflections on the Virtue of Sacrifice

"So be imitators of God, as beloved children, and live in love, as Christ loved us and handed himself over for us as a sacrificial offering to God for a fragrant aroma"
—Ephesians 5: 1-2.

"If we only knew how God regards this sacrifice, we would wish our lives to be present at a single Mass"
—St. Pio of Pietrelcina.

"Let us remember that love lives through sacrifice, and it is nourished by giving. Without sacrifice, there is no love"
—St. Maximilian Kolbe.

"The charity of the good knows no creed and is confined to no one place" —St. Marianne Cope.

"There is no place for selfishness and no place for fear! Do not be afraid when love makes demands. Do not be afraid when love requires sacrifice" —St. John Paul II.

"Martyrdom is a grace which I do not think I deserve. But if God accepts the sacrifice of my life, may my blood be a seed of freedom and a sign that hope will soon be a reality"
—St. Oscar Romero.

Avalanche of Grace!

Day 23 – Prayer for the Virtue of Sacrifice

Read God's Word: John 6: 22-71

O Father, Giver of all life!
O Jesus, One, True and Perfect Sacrifice for all!
O Holy Spirit, with Mary, You birthed the Sacrifice!

Holy Trinity, I wish to be a living sacrifice:
in thought, when love asks for selfless actions;
in silence, when self-preservation words are futile;
in speech, when justice for the other demands;
in giving, when the Giver knocks on my heart;
in conduct, when moral depravity pervades;
in home, when sin needs to be rectified;
in work, when humility cries to love relentlessly;
in private, when prayers weave many rose crowns;
in Mass, when Jesus *re-presents* His living sacrifice;
and, in suffering, when hope shows, "God is alive."

O Father, I present my body as a living sacrifice!
O Jesus, I unite my sacrifices with Your Sacrifice!
O Holy Spirit, I need more courage to die for Jesus!

Day 23 – A Story of Virtuous Sacrifice

Lev [not her real name] said, "I was once upon a time a Pentecostal minister. But, I backslid, and I got re-baptized two years ago at a Baptist church."

"Sure 'preciate what you are doing for me," Lev said many times throughout our day and a half of volunteer repair work at her trailer. "My husband was a carpenter so I know it is hard work. I used to help him when I could." Lev helped us, too. Her sacrifice of constant gratitude when we were exhausted felt like Jesus Himself thanking us and saying, "My foster father, St. Joseph, was a carpenter so I know it is tough. I used to help him when I could." Then, Lev told us, "I spent all my money raising my grandson." We let that sit with us. She undertook Jesus' poverty.

Lev, then, offered a book to me by Kathy Troccoli. "She is Catholic," she said, wishing to show respect for our Catholicity. [My research later did not indicate that Troccoli was this or that.] I scanned it and told her I liked some stories, so she told me to keep it.

Then, after our closing prayer, she gave us each an ice-cream sandwich. I did not dare ask if she *gave it all* for us.

Jesus: "My child, your little sacrifices affect souls."

I: "Jesus, I wish to be faithful in the smaller sacrifices."

Day 24 – Virtue of Holy Indifference
The Final Martyrdom

The Mother of the Maccabees witnessed the suffering, torture, and death of her seven sons with her own eyes. Then she herself underwent the same martyrdom. What strength of body, mind, and soul! What purity and fortitude of conscience!

In a word, what great love this Mother really had for God and the eternal salvation of her sons! Now she and her sons are bathed in God's heavenly glory for all eternity. …

Holy Indifference to the Max

The passage of the Maccabees presents the concept of *Holy Indifference* to the max, to the highest degree — to prefer even death over breaking the Holy Law of God. On the surface, this passage may seem to be extreme, but in the eyes of God it is not.

Holy Indifference means, in its essence, that we are called to love God with all our heart, mind, soul, and strength (Lk 10:27), even to the point of sacrificing our physical life for love of God and neighbor. Of course Jesus' death on the cross on Good Friday is by far the best example ever of the utter profundity and depths of *Holy Indifference*.

Ignatian Four Categories of Indifference

In all of these categories, the willful choosing and ardent desire of *willing what God wills* is the prevailing theme! The motivating cause is love of God and trust in His promises!

1) We should not prefer long life over a short life.

These seven sons of the Mother in 2 Maccabees were not elderly, but young. Their life was given by God and ended by obedience to God's holy will! In *The Imitation of Christ,* Thomas Kempis asserts: *"It is not important a long life, but a holy life."*

2) We should not prefer health over sickness.

In this passage from 2 Maccabees, it was not an instance of health or sickness; rather, in the case of the seven sons and their loving Mother it was a rejection of comfort and ease and a choosing of suffering and torture for the salvation of their immortal souls. We can see this in the death of Jesus on the cross and His Mother Mary standing at the foot of the cross. (Jn 19)

3) We should not prefer riches over poverty.

Most likely, if the Mother and sons were to have capitulated to the desires and whims of the King, he would have given them security. However, their security and strength was in God, their rock and their fortress!

"Our help is in the name of the Lord who made heaven and earth." (Ps 124:8)

4) We should not prefer honors over humiliations

Beyond the shadow of a doubt, all of the sons were humiliated, both in word and deed, by their martyrdom. If they were to have given in, there is a good chance they would have been honored by the King. But no! The seven sons and the Mother in 2 Maccabees willfully chose humiliations to the point of death so as to be honored by God, the *Lord of Lords and King of Kings,* for all eternity!

(Excerpt from Fr. Ed Broom's "What the 2 Maccabees Can Teach Us about Holy Indifference?".)

Avalanche of Grace!

Day 24 – Reflections on the Virtue of Holy Indifference

"Jesus said, "No one who sets a hand to the plow and looks to what was left behind is fit for the kingdom of God"
—Luke 9: 62.

"I am a nobody. I am a small rope, a tiny ladder, the tail end of a leaf"—St. Juan Diego.

"There is nothing more pleasing to God, than to see a soul who patiently and serenely bears whatever crosses it is sent"
—St. Alphonsus Liguori.

"Do not wish to be anything but what you are, and try to be that perfectly"—St. Francis de Sales.

"For Jesus Christ I am prepared to suffer still more"
—St. Maximilian Kolbe.

"I am a Catholic man and a priest. In that faith I have lived and in that faith I intend to die"—St. Edmund Campion.

"I die but God does not die. Viva Cristo Rey!"
—Blessed Anacleto Gonzalez Flores.

"Those who carry God in their hearts bear heaven wherever they go"— St. Ignatius of Loyola.

Day 24 – Prayer for the Virtue of Holy Indifference

Read God's Word: Mark 10:17-31

O Father, Most Holy, You carry me in Your Heart!
O Jesus, Holy One of Israel, help me bear my cross!
O Holy Spirit, Sanctifier, You purify my will!

O Holy Trinity, endue me with holy indifference.
I am nobody – just a child of my Father.
I offer my heart, body, and soul wholly to You.
I want to die for You so to live eternally with You.
I give up my health to suffer for You.
I take on poverty and renounce riches for You.
I have no desire to look back in choosing you, daily.
I choose to live Catholic and I will to die Catholic.
I choose to bear everything You send patiently.

O Jesus, You choose my martyrdom – white or red!

O Father, I want to carry heaven in my heart!
O Jesus, I unite my life and death with Yours!
O Holy Spirit, I rise with Jesus, Whom You rose!

Day 24 – A Story of Virtuous Holy Indifference

In the spring of 2001, when Ann first met John in his hospital room at Tufts New England Medical to give him Holy Communion, he seemed disinterested. "OK, you can give me communion" is what he said in a tone that told her that either Jesus or she or both of them were being tolerated.

Ann opened with the "Our Father," and then prayed, "This is the Lamb of God who takes away the sins of the world. Happy are those who are called to His supper." John responded, "Lord, I am not worthy to receive You, but only say the word and I shall be healed." [Yes, the old translation.] He received and they both prayed silently for a few moments. Ann saw him for many weeks after that, recognizing each time that John was becoming more serene and peaceful. Meanwhile, John received the Sacrament of Reconciliation when the chaplain priest came around.

One day when Ann walked in, John said, "Miss, I want to thank you very much for bringing me Jesus. I will be going home. The doctors have done what they could." John knew in his heart that the Lord was calling him home for his Eternal Communion with Jesus.

Jesus: "My child, offer your life and death to me."

I: "Jesus, help me prefer Your will in life and death!"

Day 25 – Virtue of Solidarity

The principle of solidarity, also articulated in terms of "friendship" or "social charity," is a direct demand of human and Christian brotherhood.[45]

An error, "today abundantly widespread, is disregard for the law of human solidarity and charity, dictated and imposed both by our common origin and by the equality in rational nature of all men, whatever nation they belong to. This law is sealed by the sacrifice of redemption offered by Jesus Christ on the altar of the Cross to his heavenly Father, on behalf of sinful humanity."[46]

Solidarity is manifested in the first place by the distribution of goods and remuneration for work. It also presupposes the effort for a more just social order where tensions are better able to be reduced and conflicts more readily settled by negotiation.

Socio-economic problems can be resolved only with the help of all the forms of solidarity: solidarity of the poor among themselves, between rich and poor, of workers among themselves, between employers and employees in a business, solidarity among nations and peoples. Inter-national solidarity is a requirement of the moral order; world peace depends in part upon this.

The virtue of solidarity goes beyond material goods. In spreading the spiritual goods of the faith, the

Church has promoted, and often opened new paths for, the development of temporal goods as well. And so, throughout the centuries has the Lord's saying been verified: "Seek first his kingdom and his righteousness, and all these things shall be yours as well":[47]

> For two thousand years this sentiment has lived and endured in the soul of the Church, impelling souls then and now to the heroic charity of monastic farmers, liberators of slaves, healers of the sick, and messengers of faith, civilization, and science to all generations and all peoples for the sake of creating the social conditions capable of offering to everyone possible a life worthy of man and of a Christian.[48]

(Catechism of the Catholic Church 1939-1942)

Day 25 – Reflections on the Virtue of Solidarity

"For in one Spirit, we were all baptized into one body, whether Jews or Greeks, slaves or free persons, and we were all given to drink of one Spirit" — 1 Corinthians 12: 13.

"True friendship consists in mutually perfecting one another and drawing close to God" — St. Teresita of the Andes.

"There is no true peace without fairness, truth, justice, and solidarity" — St. John Paul II.

"To be just, it is not enough to restrain from injustice. One must go further and refuse to play its game, substituting love for self-interest, as the driving force for society"
— St. Pedro Arrupe.

"Love is a fruit in season at all times, and within reach of every hand" — St. Teresa of Calcutta.

"Love everyone and trust His Providence, and you will find peace. I have tried it and assure you that it is so"
— Servant of God Takashi Nagai.

Avalanche of Grace!

Day 25 – Prayer for the Virtue of Solidarity

Read God's Word: Acts 2: 1-47

O Father, One with Jesus and the Holy Spirit!
O Jesus, One with the Father and the Holy Spirit!
O Holy Spirit, One with the Father and Jesus!

O Holy Trinity, model of solidarity, grace us with:
true knowledge of all our common origin;
true acceptance of equality in our rational nature;
true trust in Jesus' one sacrifice on the cross for all;
true distribution of goods and opportunities for all;
true social, economic, and political order for all;
true global peace for all;
and, true unity in Christ through prayer for all.

O Jesus, liberator of those in bondage, deliver us!
O Jesus, pour out greater faith in our hearts to heal!
O Jesus, increase in all the grace of heroic charity!

O Father, in solidarity, You gave us Jesus!
O Jesus, in loving friendship, You saved us!
O Holy Spirit, in charity, help us act justly!

Day 25 – A Story of Virtuous Solidarity

At the Vietnamese refugee camp, *solidarity* took on much meaning. As a volunteer teacher, I walked in on my first day to teach English. "Some are Buddhists, some are Catholic, some are agnostic, and others are atheists. They are headed for Sweden, Canada, and the United States," my supervisor, Chris, said. I recognized him as a fellow Catholic, from the same parish – 25 miles away. *Solidarity of mission.*

The youngest student was five and the oldest 35. The class welcomed me with joy as they hungered for connections with the outside world. They had a thirst for English skills and joked in the language they were acquiring. All were shabbily dressed but knew that together they would survive. After all, they already had, in a boat. *Solidarity for life.*

One afternoon, Mei Tran, a student about twelve, invited me to her family's home for tea. My heart broke when I saw how a family of four had only six by nine feet of living space, with all the family's bags acting as wall partitions between them and their neighbors under one big tent. *Solidarity in sharing.*

Jesus: "My child, I am hidden behind the face of every refugee."

I: "Jesus, help me be compassionate to every soul."

Avalanche of Grace!

Day 26 – Virtue of Kindness and Goodness

Kindness starts with *caring* – being tenderhearted and compassionate toward others. If God wants us to be kind to animals, how much more to people! (See Proverbs 12:10). ...Next, we must make it our goal and habit to be actively looking for opportunities to show kindness. When we see one, we need to act quickly. ...

The Greek word for "kind" is *chrestos*. Part of its meaning is *useful*, which makes it clear that biblical kindness involves *action*. "Dear children, let us stop just saying we love each other; *let us really show it by our actions*" (1 John 3:18, New Living Translation, emphasis added throughout). Action includes some kind of *self-sacrifice* and therefore *generosity* on our part, especially of our time. ...Of course, the emphasis on deeds over mere words does not mean words are unnecessary. Action *includes words*. Encouraging words of comfort, courtesy, compliments, and even correction can be heartwarming acts of kindness. ...What to say and not say should be guided by awareness of the sensitivities of others. We must help people *heal* from their emotional wounds rather than rubbing salt in those wounds. Sadly, when people know what "buttons to push," they often use that insight to further hurt each other. ...Our motive for "charitable deeds" should not be to impress people (Matthew 6:1-4). The greatest rewards from God come when our acts of kindness are done humbly, quietly and, when practical, anonymously. ...In the Bible, the "goodness" of God often refers to His gracious generosity in providing abundantly for humanity's needs and benefits (Psalms 23:6; 65:11). It can also refer to God's generous mercy and patience that allow more time for sinners to repent (Romans 2:4).

But God's goodness is much more than those things. It is *the very essence of God's nature* – His righteousness and holiness. In Ephesians 5:9, we see that His goodness is closely associated with *righteousness* and *truth*. To the extent that we have God's goodness, we have godliness or God-likeness....Jesus wants His disciples to "bear much fruit" (John 15:8). Being fruitful requires *action* – knowing the right thing to do and then *doing* it. As James wrote, *"Be doers of the word"* (James 1:22). Simply abstaining from evil and *doing nothing* is not good enough. ...Jesus "went about doing good" (Acts 10:38). We should too! "Through love, *serve one another,"* we are told (Galatians 5:13). Jesus' parable of the sheep and goats shows that God knows how much we love Him by how much we are showing self-sacrificing love for other people (Matthew 25:31-46).

Good works include *obeying* God's *laws*. God gives His Holy Spirit "to those who obey Him" (Acts 5:32). That doesn't mean salvation can be *earned* by obedience. We are saved by God's grace, which "is the gift of God" (Ephesians 2:8). However, we are being "created in Christ Jesus *for good works*" (verse 10).... He who loves God will gladly demonstrate that love for God by keeping His commandments (1 John 5:3; 2 John 6)! ... It takes courage to obey God, because it often brings persecution: "But when you do good and suffer, if you take it patiently," God will greatly bless you (1 Peter 2:20; compare Matthew 5:10).

(Excerpts from Don Hooser's *"Kindness from the Heart to the Helping Hand"* and *"Goodness: God's Character and Humanity's Potential."*)

Day 26 – Reflections on the Virtue of Kindness and Goodness

"Trust in the Lord and do good; dwell in the land and enjoy safe pasture" — Psalm 37: 3.

"A good deed is never lost, he who sows courtesy reaps friendship, and he who plants kindness gathers love"
—St. Basil the Great.

"Be kind to your wife always" —St. Homobonus.

"In every young person, a point of goodness is accessible and it is the primary duty of the educator to discover that sensitive cord of the heart so as to draw out the best in the young person"
—St. John Bosco.

"Kindness is the natural fruit of goodness of the heart"
— St. Katherine Drexel.

"Because evil has no capital of its own, it is a parasite that feeds on goodness" — Blessed Fulton J. Sheen.

"Goodness in the face of evil must suffer; for when love meets sin it will be crucified" —Blessed Fulton J. Sheen.

"The devil is afraid when we are humble and good"
—St. Anthony de Padua.

Avalanche of Grace!

Day 26 – Prayer for the Virtue of Kindness and Goodness

Read God's Word: Galatians 5: 1-26

O Father, You fed us with manna in the desert!
O Jesus, Good Shepherd, You lead us to pastures!
O Holy Spirit, River, You flow with goodness!

O *Abba*, let Your goodness and kindness
fall down anew every morning into my soul –
I trust in Your Providence for other souls, too.

O Good Shepherd, let Your goodness and kindness
be branded on the ears, eyes and heart of my soul –
I trust in Your Shepherding of other souls, too.

O Living Waters, let Your goodness and kindness
rush into all the chambers of my heart and soul –
I trust in Your Outpouring into other souls, too.

O Father, I want to be good and kind to all!
O Jesus, I want to love my enemies!
O Holy Spirit, I want Christ's light to shine on all!

Avalanche of Grace!

Day 26 – A Story of Virtuous Kindness and Goodness

The St. Paul Street Evangelization team desired to clothe and feed the homeless with hearts like Jesus. They placed a pocket Bible, reading glasses, a blanket, toothpaste and a toothbrush, pairs of socks and gloves, and a scarf in each bag. Chicken sandwiches, pudding, and water were packed to distribute to those who were hungry. They offered to pray with each person and gave rosaries and miraculous medals to all.

One homeless lady who had just come on the bus from Brooklyn voraciously ate her sandwich. A man with mismatched gloves pointed to another homeless person, and said, "She needs help more than me." Yet another was thankful for the Bible and reading glasses given so he could feed on the word of God. Still another prayed with the evangelists, signing himself with the sign of the cross, and reciting the *Our Father* and *Hail Mary* with them. He said, "I was an altar server when I was growing up." It broke the evangelists' hearts to know that someone who once served God faithfully at Mass was now homeless.

Still, they went home glorifying God, for they had received more than they could ever have given.

Jesus: "My child, I am by nature good and kind."

I: "Jesus, let Your goodness and kindness reside in me."

Avalanche of Grace!

Day 27 – Virtue of Respect for Life

As Pope Francis recently observed, almost all our problems and woes can be traced back to a loss of reverence for the sacredness and dignity of human life. ...Think about it: drugs, war, unjust economic systems, crime, violence, oppression of people, family dysfunction, sexual harassment and abuse...all start from a degradation of the innate value of the divine gift of human life.

The Holy Father has been eloquent in weaving all these together, prophetically advocating that a sensitivity towards the tender frailty of human life at *all* stages, from conception to natural death, from the pre-born baby in the womb to grandma close to death, is essential to a civilized, humane culture. ...And, he elaborates, the more vulnerable the life, the more imperative it is for people of decency and virtue to protect and defend it.

We are *pro-life*, not just *pro-birth*. As my heroic predecessor, Cardinal Terence Cooke, wrote—as he neared his own painful death from cancer—human life is no less sacred when it is vulnerable, weak, or considered "inconvenient."...No surprise, then, that Pope Francis has often spoken up for the most defenseless, the civil rights of the baby in the womb. He just recently got headlines for comparing abortion to hiring a "hit man," a "contract killer" to dispose of a life considered worthless or in-the-way.

Avalanche of Grace!

It's complicated for a person motivated not only by civic duty but by faith to figure out how to vote. We're faced with some candidates who are with us on the sacredness of the human lives of immigrants, the poor, sick, aged, and those on death row, but seem callous in ignoring the tiny life of the baby in the womb. Likewise does it make us cringe when our heroic allies in the defense of the pre-born baby, however extraordinary in this state—seem less than with us in their lack of solicitude for the lives of refugees and immigrants.

I make no apologies for prioritizing solicitude for the unborn. If we get that wrong, we're hardly credible on the other burning issues. If we allow the helpless life of the baby in the sanctuary of the mother's womb to be thrown away, it's tough to defend the lives of others who might be considered inconvenient or expendable.

How clear it is that the Holy Father's powerful lesson that *all* human life deserves reverence—at the border, in war, in the structuring of a just society, on death row—is not at the expense of softening our efforts to mute our embrace of the most threatened, marginalized, and vulnerable of them all—the baby in the womb.
(Excerpt from Cardinal Timothy Dolan's *"Lack of Respect for Life Leads to Other Problems."*)

The *Catechism of the Catholic Church* in brief says this:

> In [God's] hand is the life of every living thing and the breath of all mankind (Job 12:10).
>
> Every human life, from the moment of conception until death, is sacred because the human person has been willed for its own sake in the image and likeness of the living and holy God.
>
> The murder of a human being is gravely contrary to the dignity of the person and the holiness of the Creator.
>
> The prohibition of murder does not abrogate the right to render an unjust aggressor unable to inflict harm. Legitimate defense is a grave duty for whoever is responsible for the lives of others or the common good. From its conception, the child has the right to life.
>
> Direct abortion, that is, abortion willed as an end or as a means, is a "criminal" practice (*GS* 27 § 3), gravely contrary to the moral law. The Church imposes the canonical penalty of excommunication for this crime against human life.
>
> Because it should be treated as a person from conception, the embryo must be defended in its integrity, cared for, and healed like every other human being.
>
> Intentional euthanasia, whatever its forms or motives, is murder. It is gravely contrary to the dignity of the human person and to the respect due to the living God, his Creator.

Suicide is seriously contrary to justice, hope, and charity. It is forbidden by the fifth commandment.

Scandal is a grave offense when by deed or omission it deliberately leads others to sin gravely.

Because of the evils and injustices that all war brings with it, we must do everything reasonably possible to avoid it. The Church prays: "From famine, pestilence, and war, O Lord, deliver us."

"The arms race is one of the greatest curses on the human race and the harm it inflicts on the poor is more than can be endured" (*GS* 81 § 3).

(Catechism of the Catholic Church 2318-2329)

Day 27 – Reflections on the Virtue of Respect for Life

"Those who oppress the poor revile their Maker, but those who are kind to the needy honor him" —Proverbs 14:31.

"Abortion is profoundly anti-women. Three quarters of its victims are women: half the babies and all the mothers" —St. Teresa of Calcutta.

"The hospital is the house of God where the voices of the sick are music from heaven" —St. Camillus de Lellis.

"The young must respect their elders and the elders must love the young" —St. Benedict of Nursia.

"The right of a child is equal to the right of the mother's life. Doctors can't decide. It is a sin to kill in the womb" — St. Gianna Beretta Molla.

"Everyone who breathes, high and low, educated and ignorant, young and old, man and woman, has a mission, has a work. God sees every one of us; He creates every soul, for a purpose" —St. John Neumann.

"Christ said, 'I am the Truth.' He did not say, 'I am the custom'" —St. Toribio Romo Gonzalez.

Avalanche of Grace!

Day 27 – Prayer for the Virtue of Respect for Life

Read God's Word: Matthew 2: 1-23

O Father, You are the author of life!
O Jesus, in Your resurrection, You gave us new life!
O Holy Spirit, Your breath restores our broken lives!

O Father, You alone can give and take life.
O Father, You alone infuses a soul into each baby.
O Father, You alone have a mission for each soul.

O Jesus, You alone are Savior to each soul.
O Jesus, You alone are Healer of souls' wounds.
O Jesus, You alone are Atonement for souls' sins.

O Holy Spirit, You alone are Helper of the soul.
O Holy Spirit, You alone are Advocate for the soul.
O Holy Spirit, You alone are Comforter to the soul.

O Father, protect all human life from womb to tomb!
O Jesus, save all souls from the enemy!
O Holy Spirit, grace souls to cherish life!

Day 27 – A Story of Virtuous Respect for Life

They shared stories about abortion; some sacrificed, some gave in, and some did not know any better.

Medical doctor: "First day at a clinic, I did not realize this but, in the middle of the night, an abortion was about to happen in a back room. I was appalled and left the job. I refused the just wages they wished to give me for a day's work."

LPN: "I walked out after I heard an aborted baby kicking in the trash can. It was so wrong. That could have been my baby."

Counselor: "She chose to abort her baby at five months because her boyfriend had left her a couple of weeks before. I offered prayers for the baby."

Friend to a friend: "Yes, I have four kids, but I have had five abortions. I know that it is not right. My husband is selfish and it has to be his way."

Woman victim: "I wish someone had told me about the local home for unwed mothers and the option of adoption."

Father victim: "I only wanted what she wanted. I lost my baby. I do reparation now for my sin."

Jesus: "*My child, I am the Life within each child.*"

I: "Jesus, "*help me protect Life in all your children.*"

Day 28 – Virtue of Industry and Diligence

"If we really want to sanctify our work, we have inescapably to fulfill the first condition: that of working, and working well, with human and supernatural seriousness."[1]

We have seen, in a previous article, that working for a supernatural reason is the "soul" of the sanctification of work.[2] Now we will look at the "body" it animates: work well done. If our reason for working is truly love for God and neighbor, this necessarily entails that the job be done as well as possible.

We should especially keep in mind that, as St. Josemaria taught, sanctifying our ordinary work requires doing the work itself well, aiming to do it as perfectly as possible, and fulfilling all our professional and social obligations. It requires working conscientiously, responsibly, lovingly and perseveringly, without negligence or sloppiness.

To profit from this teaching of Opus Dei's founder, we should bear in mind that when we speak about working well we are referring above all to the *activity* involved, and not to its *outcome*.

It can happen that, in spite of our best efforts, the end product is defective, either through some unintentional mistake or through factors outside our control. In these cases, which are not uncommon, we see clearly the difference between working with a Christian outlook and being successful in a merely human sense. In the first case, it is the act of working itself which is esteemed, and although the desired object hasn't been achieved, it was done as well as possible for love of God and the desire to co-redeem with Christ, and so nothing has been wasted. Thus we don't get upset when confronted with setbacks but try to overcome them, seeing them as an opportunity to be more united to Christ's Cross. But if one is seeking primarily success, then when things don't work out well everything is regarded as a failure. Clearly, someone with this perspective will never understand what it means to sanctify professional work.

Working conscientiously means trying to do things as perfectly as possible humanly speaking, for supernatural reasons. It doesn't mean working well and afterwards adding a supernatural motive. It is much deeper than that. What leads a Christian to do things perfectly is love for God, because "it is no good offering to God something that is less perfect than our poor human limitations permit. The work that we offer must be without blemish and it must be done as carefully as possible, even in its smallest details, for God will not accept shoddy workmanship. 'You shall not offer anything that is faulty,' Holy Scripture warns us, 'because it would not be worthy of him' (Lev 22:20)."[3]

When a person tries to do things well, he is usually successful and produces a good result. Moreover, striving to sanctify one's work generally leads to professional prestige, since love for God leads one "to excel oneself gladly in duty and in sacrifice."[4] But we should never forget something that bears emphasizing: that at times God allows setbacks and failures precisely so that we purify our intention and share in Christ's Cross. And this doesn't mean that we haven't worked well and sanctified our work.

(Excerpt from reflections of St. Josemaria Escriva's "Working Conscientiously.")

Day 28 – Reflections on the Virtue of Industry and Diligence

"Go to the ant, O sluggard, study her ways and learn wisdom; for though she has no chief, no commander or ruler, she procures her food in the summer, stores up her provisions in the harvest" — Proverbs 6: 6-8.

"I can't do big things, but I want to do everything, even the smallest, for the greater glory of God" — St. Dominic Savio.

"The saints did not become saints without many a sacrifice and many a struggle" — St. Jean Marie Vianney.

"Holiness does not consist in doing more difficult things every day, but in doing them every day with greater love"
— St. Josemaria Escriva.

"Nothing seems tiresome or painful when you work for a Master who pays well; who rewards even a cup of cold water given for love of Him" — St. Dominic Savio.

"Humility is the virtue that requires the greatest amount of effort" — St. Rose Philippine Duchesne.

"If I should become sick and unable to work, then I shall be like the Lord on the Cross. He will have mercy on me and help me, I am sure" — St. Kateri Tekakwitha.

Avalanche of Grace!

Day 28 – Prayer for the Virtue of Industry and Diligence

Read God's Word: Matthew 25: 1-30

O Father, who let man toil as a result of sin!
O Jesus, who emulates what the Father does!
O Holy Spirit, present work of Jesus in the world!

O Holy Trinity, in You, may all my labors be:
sanctified with Your grace with effort on my part;
totally offered to You as an unblemished sacrifice;
done well, with greater love every day;
attentive to details and pleasing to You;
fruitful in love from start to finish;
revealing in soul so nothing may be lost even in defeat;
and, nailed to Jesus' Cross – in success and failure.

O Jesus, You worked lovingly unto death.
You said, "It is finished" when You were done, O Jesus.

O Father, like You, may I toil with love in all I do.
O Jesus, like You, may I toil until the job is done.
O Holy Spirit, in You, may I do His toil on earth.

Day 28 – A Story of Virtuous Industry and Diligence

Work ethics become virtues when moved by God. Workers offer their work to God to help them bless their own families, and help others, too. Such is the case with the Gonzalez family who asked God to sanctify their work and family.

Jose picked the fields while his wife, Henrietta, cleaned hotels during the day and washed dishes at a restaurant in the night to feed their two kids, Raul and Maria. Henrietta went to Catholic Charity's immigration and citizenship classes to learn English. She later enrolled in college, and earned her degree in Human Services. She worked her way up to becoming a Family Services Advocate.

Once established, Henrietta was able to afford a car, and send her children to college. In her career, Henrietta was also able to help other immigrants by pointing them to available support services to help them survive. She also began sending money home to her parents and family in El Salvador.

Holiness of work is *all for His greater glory*.

Jesus: *"My child, work for the greater good, always."*

I: *"Jesus, I need Your grace to give my best in work."*

Avalanche of Grace!

Day 29 – Virtue of Hospitality

Hospitality is a hidden gift among Catholics. For some reason, hospitality has now become either something someone does for one's family, or for one's work connections. Hospitality on the more formal level, which my parent's practiced well in the 1960s and 1970s, died long ago. No longer does one see wine and cheese gatherings, or intimate dinners where I learned as a child to listen to adult talk. And, most importantly, where I learned manners. Hospitality is not an option. It is a virtue and a command.

The Benedictines practice it well, still, after all these centuries, setting extra places at the convent guest house or monastery guest table in case someone drops in and needs sustenance.

What has disappeared is common hospitality among Catholics. ...Barbecues may include newcomers to the neighborhood, or new friends.

Chapter One — What Is Hospitality?

The act of being friendly and welcoming may seem like a simple gesture, but this entails one of the greatest virtues missing in today's society—that of trust. To trust other human beings, one must be in a trust relationship with God, with one's companions on the way to heaven, such as members of one's family or church. Trust implies that one sees the goodness in the other, not merely the negative aspects of that person's character or personality. All people, as we know, or at least heard once in our lives, reflect Christ in some way.

Let me give an example of the type of trust which would lead to hospitality. Friends of friends invited me to their home for a week so that I could look for property a while ago. I had never met this couple, although we had lived in the same city, and had mutual friends. Their home was open to me while I visited places in their area, as they had moved to another city, where I was considering moving. Although we had never met, I experienced one of the most comfortable and loving weeks in my recent history. The couples hospitable actions included generosity and meeting my needs for that week. Behind their relaxed and happy manners was a deep faith in God. As older Catholics, the couple had grown up in a gentler, more "Christian" world. Even though they were savvy as to the growing darkness of the times, their faith led them to a trust and openness. In other words, they had not succumbed to the present danger of cynicism.

Hospitality is thinking of the other, creating an environment so that the person feels at home. My extended definition of hospitality would include the openness to praying together, such as inviting the guest to join the family rosary.

Chapter Two — Fear, time, money, stress

...Fear usually is based on unrealistic expectations, or is a reaction to a trauma. As Christians, Catholics are called to live without fear. The basic relationship to Our Father, God, is one of a trusting child. Such saints as St. Therese of Lisieux reminded us of this loving kindness the Father has toward each one of us. Trust in Divine Providence defeats fear. However, one can say without exaggeration that we in the West seem to be more and more obsessed with fear. Fear kills love.

One cannot love if one is wrapped up in fears, and such fears can lead to a mental digging of the moat, putting the crocodile in the moat, pulling up the drawbridge and double locking the door. Yes, society is more dangerous. Catholics have always lived in danger, of some sort.

In this great country of Britain, one only has to read the stories of the martyrs during the recusant times to be reminded of dangerous times. However, families opened their doors to the seminary priests to say Mass, and even stay in their houses, in the face of a horrific death for doing so. Hospitality did not die because of the fear of punishment, Or, did it? I wonder if fear still holds many Catholics in bondage, to the point where they cannot open their doors or contemplate being hospitable.

A second problem may be time. So many of us work long hours and commute to our jobs. In opposition to this complaint of some who hold that they do not have time to be hospitable, I think of my ancestors on the small farms, working extremely long hours, and pulling themselves out of poverty, yet having others in for dinner, for talk, even sharing musical evenings. Time is a gift to be used wisely. Can we not make time for the guest, the stranger? One thinks of the many stories of the saints who entertained a guest only to have that guest reveal himself as Christ, or an angel. Do we not have a phrase, perhaps being lost as the memory of hospitality is lost, that one never knows if one is entertaining angels?

Time must be made for the "other", or we risk the chance of not being open to Christ Himself. What about the complaint that it cost too much to entertain, to be hospitable. My answer is this, Share what one has. If one has tea and biscuits, one can still invite a person in. If one has coffee and biscotti, that is enough to start a friendship, a meaningful conversation. If one has a rosary, one can invite another to prayer. ...

Dinners are not the only venue for hospitality, although I think dinners are the best way to share and be friendly. One does not have to show off and have the "best" of food, only what one usually eats. Hospitality is not a competition as to who serves the best, but an opening of the heart and mind to another.

...True hospitality takes place in the ordinary eating of one's home meals, the opening up of one's space, the sharing of one's time. It is too easy to ignore hospitality when one is eating out all the time. At one time in my life, I was guilty of eating out too much and thinking that going out with a friend was the same as hospitality in the home. It is not.

What about finances? Money does not have to be an issue. ...Simple, warm, friendly. Tea, sweets, conversation surrounded by the host, hostess and children.

What about stress? Some acquaintances tell me they are too stressed to be hospitable. ...Setting aside one's self, called "dying to self" among Catholics, is the very thing to beat stress. When one reaches out and forgets self, problems can seem trivial.

Chapter Three — The Call to Evangelize

In Romans 12:13, Paul reminds the Catholics of their duties — "Communicating to the necessities of the saints. Pursuing hospitality."

These are commands, not "extras." Perhaps the older customs of Abraham were dying out in the Roman Empire. Perhaps the Gentiles to whom Paul was writing needed reminding of their duties.

"Pursuing hospitality" is not waiting for it to happen. This directive from the great Apostle to the Gentiles indicates that all of us must go out of our way to create times and venues for hospitality. A lovely time together getting to know each other in a homey atmosphere can easily lead to discussions about God. ...

Many people today decry the decline of the Church, and Church membership, especially here in Europe. Could one reason be simply that we have put up the drawbridge and locked our doors?

"See how they love one another…." is a cry which would be difficult to hear in many Catholic circles. In John13:35, the Evangelist tells us, "By this shall all men know that you are my disciple, if you love one another."

Does the world see us loving each other? Are we open about our love of God and love of neighbor? Hospitality can create bonds of love. Such bonds of love lead to conversion. This is your job and mine. … Evangelization. The open door is one key way to bring souls to Christ.

(Excerpts from Jay Toups' "Catholic Hospitality" as found in *Catholic, Catholic Social Doctrine, and Generosity*.)

Avalanche of Grace!

Day 29 – Reflections on the Virtue of Hospitality

"Be hospitable to one another without complaining. As each one has received a gift, use it to serve one another as good stewards of God's varied grace" — 1 Peter 4:9.

"Let no one ever come to you without leaving better or happier. Be the living expression of God's kindness: kindness in your face, kindness in your eyes, kindness in your smile"
—St. Teresa of Calcutta.

"God's love for us is not greater in heaven than it is now"
—St. Thomas Aquinas.

"Listen with the ear of your heart" —St. Benedict of Nursia.

"Let go of your plans" —St. Edith Stein.

"Love the poor, through them thou wilt find mercy"
—St. Isaac the Syrian.

"Be attentive to the voice of grace"
—St. Elizabeth Ann Seton.

"Hold your eyes on God and leave the doing to Him"
—St. Jane de Chantal.

Avalanche of Grace!

Day 29 – Prayer for the Virtue of Hospitality

Read God's Word: Luke 19: 1-27

O Father, Father of the poor, alien, and widow!
O Jesus, Friend to the sinner, leper, and paralytic!
O Holy Spirit, Heart of love and hospitality to all!

O Holy Trinity, let gentleness arise in me when:
visitors call on me, for You, Lord, are the guest;
You appear as hurt, bereaving, or wounded souls;
what to serve concerns me more than whom I serve;
tidying the house for guests overrides being present;
interactions are serious rather than lighthearted;
and, guests are impolite, strange, or just different.

O Jesus, Perfect Host, increase trust in me for all!
O Jesus, Perfect Host, let me see You in my guests!
O Jesus, Perfect Host, let my guests be healed!

O Father, open my heart to all seeking You!
O Jesus, open my heart to the poor, sick and needy!
O Holy Spirit, let my hearth be Your Heart for all!

Day 29 – A Story of Virtuous Hospitality

Mel was eager to visit Leela's home for the Festival of Lights. After all, Leela was a guest at Mel's family home for Christmas. Both were fifteen.

Leela was happy to just receive Mel as a guest — not ashamed of her lowly space, and not making excuses for her bare furniture.

No parents, no siblings. No cookies, no coffee, no tea, and no juice. Just water. Leela's eyes danced with joy as she asked Mel more about herself. Unreservedly, Mel talked about her background, dreams and ambitions of becoming a Math teacher. Leela, in turn, shared that she hoped to one day work as a receptionist.

Mel learned what true hospitality is. Leela had received her with smiles and a cheery heart. Mel deeply felt in her heart that someone her age had truly listened to her. Mel encountered *Christ in the stranger*, in a Hindu, who showed her how to be Christ-like in hospitality, and how to engage in a conversation.

Jesus: "My child, listen to people, for I am there, too."

I: "Jesus, help me listen and see You in the stranger."

Avalanche of Grace!

Day 30 – Virtue of Magnanimity

Humility and Magnanimity for Thomas Aquinas

...The work of 13th century Dominican friar, Thomas Aquinas, remains a touchstone for many contemporary virtue ethicists. In writing his greatest work, the *Summa Theologiae*, Thomas used the best of human knowledge at the time, confident that there could be no ultimate contradiction between truths. His principal sources were Augustinian (therefore Platonic) Christianity, and Aristotelian philosophy. Along the way he cites authorities ranging from the Romans, Cicero … . He does not shrink from disagreeing with his sources when necessary, but his genius lies in his ability to synthesize without syncretism.

However, humility was a problem. From Augustine, Thomas inherited a strong vision of humility as a central virtue for Christians. For Augustine, humility involved seeing oneself as a broken sinner utterly worthless apart from the grace of God in Christ. With his high doctrine of the power of God's grace to rescue the sinner, Augustine recognized no limit to our virtuous self-abasement, so we might know more clearly our need for that saving grace.… Enter Aristotle, the pagan, the other main source. Thomas had already stepped away from Augustine's negative assessment of the virtues of non-Christians, asserting that the non-believer's moral virtues remain truly good, even if limited to the natural (or secular) sphere. But on the virtue of humility, Aristotle contradicts Augustine. Aristotle described a virtue of humility and magnanimity in spiritual guidance magnanimity, or "great-souledness," which invites us to strive to do the best we can in life, in accordance with a true assessment of our gifts. For Aristotle, all virtues exist between two vices, one which looks like "too much" of a given virtue, the other looks like a deficit. The vice of "too much" magnanimity is stupid vainglory, by which we try to do things that are beyond our abilities and look foolish. ...The vice of too little magnanimity is "undue humility," which Aristotle warned was the worse of the two vices, since it will lead us to fail to accomplish what good we can. So Augustine praises humility and Aristotle condemns it. How would these fit together?

Thomas wrestles with the relationship between these two virtues over and over in the *Summa*, changing his stance as he goes [6]. ...

The mode of humility is restraint—it pulls us back from a natural inclination to see ourselves as better than others, to attribute our accomplishments to our own efforts only, or to see ourselves not in need of God's grace. Most people err in the direction of excessive self-regard, and are called to practice restraint. This is where some of the pernicious mis-definitions of humility arise: while most of us might need to moderate our self regard, the extreme version of this kind of practice would be self-abasement, denial of our own good gifts, or accepting being kept in a down-trodden status. So the vices that bracket humility are these: not enough humility is blind pride-fulness, while what looks like "too much" humility is self-abasement that yields spiritual self-destruction, not flourishing.

Hence the final part of my definition is crucial: humility is cultivated by the practice of other-centeredness. It invites us to open our eyes to see the great things God is doing in other people's lives and what other people are accomplishing in other circumstances. To be humble is to appreciate that there are excellences in other fields that, if I turn my attention to them, will deepen and broaden my vision of life. Rick Warren caught it well: "Humility is not thinking less of yourself, it's thinking of yourself less."

Magnanimity's mode is encouragement. Magnanimity urges us to make the best of the gifts God has given us. Beyond mere self-understanding, this requires devotion and effort. Consider the countless hours of practice that contributes to a virtuoso musical performance, or the miles and miles run by a marathoner in training. While some of us naturally overreach, most of us need a little push to work hard to "be all we can be." To practice magnanimity, then, is to work to recognize the gifts we have; to see how we need to work to perfect them for the good of all. If humility invites us to see and value others' gifts, magnanimity requires that we see, and value, our own intrinsic worth as human beings, and to act from a position of healthy self-love. To fail in magnanimity is to be pusillanimous, "small-souled," which implies a timid, lazy, or socially-imposed reluctance to "be all we can be." Consider the evil effects of internalized racism or sexism: in the face of social messages of our unworthiness, people on the wrong end of those social sins might come to believe that they can never achieve anything great, or even anything average, and then settle for less than what is due to a child of God.

Another important distinction is this: while humility and magnanimity both recognize that we receive our gifts from God, only humility calls us beyond the gifts/weakness calculus to ponder also our context as creatures. the pride that humility opposes, then, is of two sorts: everyday or trivial pride and a more dire vice that tempts us to disregard God entirely. Humility's two-context construal protects us from the venial pride of "my apple pie is the best on the block," (pridefully not noticing how others are contributing brilliantly in other ways—... child care, etc.), to the deadly pride which cuts us off from God altogether.

Also, I would add that humility has an epistemological role in moral life. How do we recognize what is virtuous at all? It is humility, with its characteristic act of looking outside ourselves, that invites us to recognize, value, and seek to acquire virtues that we might otherwise ignore. It is this kind of humility that calls us to see how "Christ plays in ten thousand places." It is humility that helps us to see virtues where we might not recognize them at all, and is fundamental to the basic Christian call to look to the outcast, the poor, and the marginalized not just as preferential objects of our care, but as contributing to our ideals for Christian living. ...

[In sum]...a central virtue in Christian tradition, humility calls us to be alert to God's manifold presence in the world; counteracting foolish narcissism. Magnanimity is the devoted and resolute cultivation of our own excellence. The two virtues differ in mode (restraint versus encouragement), object (other's gifts versus our own), and motive (both recognize that our gifts come from God, but only humility has the larger role of keeping us mindful of our need for God).

(Excerpt from Lisa Fullam's "Humility and Magnanimity in Spiritual Guidance," 40-43.)

Day 30 – Reflections on the Virtue of Magnanimity

"One person is lavish yet grows still richer; another is too sparing, yet is the poorer. Whoever confers benefits will be amply enriched, and whoever refreshes others will be refreshed" — Proverbs 11: 24-25.

"However great the work God may achieve by an individual, [the person] must not indulge in self-satisfaction. He ought, rather, to be all the more humbled, seeing himself merely as a tool, which God has made use of" — St. Vincent de Paul.

"When we attend to the needs of those in want, we give them what is theirs, not ours. More than performing works of mercy, we are paying a debt of justice" — St. Gregory the Great.

"[T]he rosary prayer rises like incense to the feet of the Almighty. Mary responds at once like a beneficial dew, bringing new life to human hearts" — St. Therese Lisieux.

"Our true worth, does not consists in what human beings think of us. What we really are consists in what God wants us to be" — St. John Berchmans.

"God the Father gathered all the waters and called them the seas. He gathered all His graces and called them Mary"
— St. Louis de Montfort.

Avalanche of Grace!

Day 30 – Prayer for the Virtue of Magnanimity

Read God's Word: 1 John 3: 1-17

O Father, You lavishly gave us Your heart – Jesus!
O Jesus, You freely gave us Your life on the cross!
O Holy Spirit, You bountifully gift us with grace!

O Trinity, I ask for Your avalanche of grace to let me be:
crucified, so that in Christ I may move and live;
open, to greatness of love in small and big ways;
big-hearted, in kindly words here and there;
benevolent, in alms for the poor and needy;
hidden, as You pour out of me, for the other;
and, radiant, as I thank You for You first loved me.

O Jesus, Greatest Gift, beyond You there is nothing!
O Jesus, Perfect Gift, You accept my lowliest gifts!
O Jesus, Holy Gift, may others become holy as You!

O Father, I desire to be as magnanimous as You!
O Jesus, I desire to pour out goodness to all!
O Holy Spirit, I desire Your fullness of grace in all!

Day 30 – A Story of Virtuous Magnanimity

Thankfulness yields stories of generous people who shared their time, treasure, or talent with the other, causing the latter to pause, emulate, and grow likewise to be benevolent.

Single mom of four children. "Priscilla offered her second home to me until my kids and I could get on our feet."

Middle child of thirteen siblings. "Timmy always shared snacks with all of us, his younger siblings, before he took some for himself."

God-daughter. "Teresita listened thoughtfully to me when I faced challenges at home, school, and later at work. Her counsel was kind and gentle."

Mom of a boy of nine. "Colby ran ahead to open doors for older ladies and men who had walkers or canes, or were in wheel-chairs."

Friend. "My best-friend Evan helped me to lose pounds by strength training and running. I lost ten pounds in two weeks and fifty pounds in three months. Now I want to help other people as he helped me."

Jesus: "My child, My overflowing heart is far-reaching."

I: "Jesus, help me to listen with Your heart and give freely."

Avalanche of Grace!

Day 31 – Virtue of Orderliness

...If you get back to the root of the word [ordinary as in Ordinary Sunday], you'll find it comes from the Latin *ordo*, which means "order." And here things start to get interesting, because one of the first things the Bible tells us about God's creative work is that he brings order out of chaos.

In the beginning, when God created the heavens and the earth—and the earth was without form or shape, with darkness over the abyss and a mighty wind sweeping over the water—then, God said: "Let there be light," and there was light. God saw that the light was good. God then separated the light from the darkness (*Gen 1:1-4).*

God does not merely have a preference for order, like we might prefer a tidy room whereas our roommate is fine with a little mess. *Order is part of who God is*. God is a rational being, which means he possesses an ordered intellect. His thoughts are not random and chaotic. This rationality of God is reflected in the order of creation.

The fact that creation is ordered means that it can be studied, which is the premise that makes science possible. Of course, to study creation, we must also have rational minds. God made man in his image (Gen 1:27). This means that, like God, we also possess a rational intellect. It means that, like God, order is part of our being.

Creatures of Habit

Whether we are conscious of it or not, we all tend to some sort of order. We are creatures of habit. We like having routine in our lives. This may not be a strict military-type routine. But most of us generally like to wake up and go to sleep around the same time each day. We have certain daily tasks and rituals, from brushing our teeth to doing daily prayers. Our growling stomachs prompt us to eat our meals on a schedule (and let us know if we miss one). Intentional or not, there is a rhythm that orders our days, weeks and months. If one is not imposed on us externally (by work or school) we naturally create our own routine — and we become unsettled when that routine gets disrupted. ...

A Call to Order

All Christians are called to order their lives to God, not just monks, nuns and clergy. All of us should ask the question, "What is my life ordered toward?" I mentioned above that we are creatures of habit. Habits can be good or bad. Good habits help to instill proper order in our lives and help us to become people of virtue. Bad habits cause our lives to be ordered toward vice and can lead us away from God.

In teaching about the moral life, the Church often uses the term *disordered* to describe any desire that is contrary to right reason. Disorder is not the same thing as chaos, which is the absence of order. Disorder means order in the wrong direction. If you are trying to drive to Canada from North Carolina by heading south, your navigation is disordered. You are not going to end up in the right place.

So lying is disordered, because our minds are made to know truth. Adultery is disordered because marriage is ordered toward fidelity. Hate is disordered, because our hearts are made to love. Every sin stems from a disordered desire in the human heart. Christ's call for repentance in the gospel, then, is a call to order. Jesus calls for a radical reordering of our lives toward God.

The first reading this Sunday (1 Kgs 19:16b, 19-21) tells of the prophet Elijah anointing Elisha as his successor. Answering this call causes Elisha to reorder his entire life. He slaughters his oxen and breaks apart his yoke and plow, symbolizing a total departure from his former way of life. He leaves his father and mother behind to follow Elijah.

We see this echoed in our gospel reading (Lk 9:51-62) when Jesus tells someone who wants to say farewell to his family before following Christ, "No one who sets a hand to the plow and looks to what was left behind is fit for the kingdom of God" (Lk 9:62). This doesn't mean telling your parents goodbye before leaving is wrong—in fact God commands us to honor our parents (Ex 20:12). But it underscores the radical reordering of our lives Jesus calls us to. Reordering our lives to Christ might involve us leaving behind things that we have strong attachments to. We need to be prepared for this as Christian disciples.

Live by the Spirit

This new order of Christian discipleship is spelled out more explicitly in this Sunday's second reading (Gal 5:1, 13-18). Without God's grace, we are ordered toward our own selfish desires, pleasures, comfort and pride. We are *disordered* because we can never find fulfillment by serving ourselves. St. Paul calls us instead to "serve one another through love" (Gal 5:13). He instructs us to "live by the Spirit and you will certainly not gratify the desires of the flesh. For the flesh has desires against the Spirit, and the Spirit against the flesh; these are opposed to each other…" (Gal 5:16-17). By "flesh" Paul doesn't just mean our physical bodies. He means our former self, before we put on Christ — who we are without God. To live by the Spirit is to live according to the divine order.

This is what Christian discipleship means. It means being ordered to the eternal mind of God as revealed in Christ, who demonstrates for us perfect love of God and love of neighbor. To be a disciple may involve leaving certain things behind—in fact it almost certainly will. And this may seem difficult, as I am sure it was difficult for Elisha to burn his plow and yoke. These were the sources of his livelihood. To let them go required great trust in God.

You and I may not be called to leave behind ox and plow, but we are each called to leave behind the "yoke of slavery" (Gal 5:1) – the sin that leaves us slaves to our own disordered desires. God did not make us for slavery, but for freedom. "For freedom Christ set us free" (Gal 5:1). Our hearts are free when they are ordered toward what is good, just as our minds are free when they are ordered toward what is true. By ordering our lives toward Christ, we begin to live in the Spirit of God, which as men and women made in his divine image, is what we were always meant to be.

(Excerpt from "The Order of Our Lives," by Deacon Matthew Newsome, Catholic campus minister at Western Carolina University, in the Diocese of Charlotte.)

Avalanche of Grace!

Day 31 – Reflections on the Virtue of Orderliness

"It was I who made the earth and created the people upon it; It was my hands that stretched out the heavens; I gave the order to all their host" —Isaiah 45: 12.

"The orderly arrangement of the whole universe is a kind of musical harmony whose maker and artist is God"
—St. Gregory of Nyssa.

"You go to pray to become a bonfire: a living flame, giving light and heat" —St. Josemaria Escriva.

"Do not allow any sadness to dwell in your soul, for sadness prevents the Holy Spirit from freely acting"
—St. Pio of Pietrelcina.

"When you decide to live a clean life, chastity will not be a burden on you: it will be a crown of triumph"
—St. Josemaria Escriva.

"Every element has a sound, an original sound from the order of God; all those sounds unite like the harmony from harps and zithers" —St. Hildegard of Bingen.

"He that made all things for love, by the same love keepeth them, and shall keep them without end" —St. Julian of Norwich.

Avalanche of Grace!

Day 31 – Prayer for the Virtue of Orderliness

Read God's Word: Genesis 1, 2, and 3

O Father, the Alpha and Omega, the First and Last!
O Jesus, You and Mary struck the serpent's head!
O Holy Spirit, Your wind swept over the waters!

O God, order my soul to Your Divine law and morality.
Father, I desire You in my soul to be the first and last
of my every intention, thought, will, action and project.
Jesus, with Mary's help, I ask for the grace
to stay steadfast to Your law and spirit of love.
Holy Spirit, may Your rustling Winds flow
over the shambolic parts of my soul to re-teach it.
I long for Your sweet beckonings
to submit to and stay in Your Gracious order.

O Jesus, O Seed of Mary, restore me to innocence,
and purity of heart in the grace of the Sacraments!

O Father, thank You for Jesus, the New Adam!
O Jesus, thank You for the New Tree of Life!
O Holy Spirit, help correct all my disordered ways!

Day 31 – A Story of Virtuous Orderliness

"I cannot get past the first chapter of Genesis," Patrick said. He struggled with this because he had strongly entrenched beliefs in Karl Marx' phrase, "Religion is the opium of the people."

But, the following summer, Patrick gave his life to Jesus at a Christian camp for college students. "I realized that He truly loved me and died for me on the cross even while I was a sinner." In time, Patrick decided to follow the one, holy, Catholic, and apostolic faith. His reason revealed how scripture led him:

> As I read the Word of God, John 6 intrigued me. Jesus is the Bread of Life and Blood of the New Covenant, for He said, "Whoever eats of my flesh and drinks my blood, has eternal life, and I will raise him up on the last day"(John 6: 54). I wanted to eat His flesh and drink His blood. I desired eternal life with Him so I found Christ's church that eats His body and drinks His blood.

Indeed, Jesus established the order of grace through the apostolic succession when He said, "Thou art Peter, and upon this rock I establish my Church..." (Matthew 16: 18).

Jesus: "My child, I want grace to flow in Your life."

I: "Jesus, etch Your order of grace into My Heart!"

Avalanche of Grace!

Day 32 – Virtue of Discernment

Where does discernment play a role in Ignatian spirituality?

Ignatian spirituality begins with the premise that God is present in every moment and every bit of matter in the universe. God wants to play a role in our every decision. Humans are called to praise, reverence and serve God through our every decision and action. Discernment of Spirits helps us to determine which actions of ours will bring about God's greater glory and also will—in the words of St. Ignatius—"help souls."

What are some distinctive features to discernment of spirits?

Probably the most surprising feature of the Ignatian approach is the premise that God's will can often be discovered in our "great desires." Much of Christian spirituality presumes that our desires are bad and will lead us to sinful actions. Ignatius believed that our problem was not desiring too much but rather desiring too little. He believed that we sin not because we've followed our desires but because our desires are "disordered." That is, the whole collection of our desires are placed in the wrong order, leaving us to follow petty, superficial desires rather than the great big desires that God has placed in our hearts. What are these "great desires?" Ultimately, they are variations of actions that will lead to faith, hope and love for God and our fellow neighbor. If we do the work of discernment in our prayer, we will discover these great desires and follow them rather than the petty, superficial ones.

What are the "Rules for Discernment" in the Spiritual Exercises of St. Ignatius?

The Rules for Discernment can be found in the appendices of the book of the Spiritual Exercises, written by St. Ignatius. There are two sets of rules: Rules for the First Week and Rules for the Second Week.

What do these Rules teach us?

They are written by Ignatius to help us determine the sources of our movements towards or away from one action or another. If these movements within us are from a good spirit—that is, a spirit that leads us ever closer to God and God's Kingdom on earth—then we will choose to follow them. If they are from a bad spirit—that is, from a spirit that leads us away from God and God's Kingdom—then we will want to ignore or resist them.

The Rules teach us that sometimes we are in a state of spiritual consolation wherein the good spirit is leading us ever closer to God and the Kingdom. Sometimes we are in a state of spiritual desolation wherein we are inclined away from God and the Kingdom. The problem is that if we do not stop and think about it, we might be in a different state than we're presuming. We might think that we're in consolation when we are in fact in desolation, or vice versa. The Rules, then, are designed to teach us to determine our present state-of-being so that we can decide what to do about it....

What are some of the graces you've experienced from your own process of discernment?

Ultimately, practicing discernment in my own life has led me to grow ever closer to God the Father and to Jesus Christ. They have helped me to notice when I'm being tempted to act based on "lower passions" such as anger, resentment, fear, lust for superficial pleasures, power-grasping and so on. Because I can better detect these movements inside of me, I can name them aloud to God and myself. Then, they don't have so much power to control me. This leaves me free to follow my "great desires," for concrete acts of faith, hope and love.

What are some of the challenges you've faced in your experience of discernment?

After you've grown more mature in the spiritual life, you are not as tempted by grave sins. You truly desire to do good. But, unfortunately, the difficult work of discernment is only just beginning. Now, you are called to discern God's *greater* glory. You are called not just to do good things but to do the best things you could possibly do—the things that will lead to the most faithful, hopeful, loving acts. The problem is that inside you is a spirit that will try to move you to lesser goods. If this false spirit can't succeed in tempting you with bad things, then it will tempt you with *less good* things. So, the great challenge is to determine what will bring about God's *greater* glory.

Another great challenge is detecting when I am in a state of "false consolation." Ignatius describes this state as a time when I believe that I am in sync with God and by all appearances, I am. But, in fact, the false spirit has led me down a blind alley. I am feeling good and even looking good to others, but I am not actually following what God is really calling me to do. Ignatius says that the false spirit can appear as an "angel of light"—that it can look like a holy movement from God when, in fact, it will lead me away from my true vocations in life. …

(Excerpt from Fr. Sean Salai S.J.'s interview with Fr. Mark Thibodeaux (interviewee), "Discerning Good and Bad Spirits: Wisdom from a Jesuit Spiritual Writer.")

Day 32 – Reflections on the Virtue of Discernment

"Beloved, do not trust every spirit but test the spirits to see whether they belong to God, because many false prophets have gone out into the world" —I John 4:1.

"Whatever you are doing, that which makes you feel most alive is where God is" —St. Ignatius of Loyola.

"Those whose hearts are pure are temples of the Holy Spirit" —St. Lucy of Syracuse.

"The blessed martyrs cry to our hearts. Believe in God who is love. Believe in Him in good times and bad. Awaken hope. May it produce in you, the fruit of fidelity to God, in every trial" —St. John Paul II.

"Believe me. No one can be truly happy in this world unless he is at peace with God" —St. John Bosco.

"Strive to preserve your heart in peace; let no event of this world disturb it" —St. John of the Cross.

"Let peace be your quest and aim" —St. Benedict of Nursia.

Avalanche of Grace!

Day 32 – Prayer for the Virtue of Discernment

Read God's Word: 1 John 3: 18–4: 6

O Father, Father of Truth, I was created for the Truth!
O Jesus, the Truth, help me be set free in the Truth!
O Holy Spirit of Truth, I want to abide in the Truth!

O Holy Trinity, help me discern spirits, believing
that God is present in every moment of my life;
and, Jesus Christ, the Son of God, became flesh.
I will praise, thank, and worship God in every decision.
I will praise, thank, and worship God in every action.
In you, my actions must speak for your greater glory.
In you, my decisions and actions must help souls.

O Jesus, I want to remain in You and You in me!
O Spirit of Grace and Truth, help me truly seek
the Living God of true consolations and desolations
and live out His most holy will.

O Father, Father of Truth, shield my soul from lies!
O Jesus, the Truth, may I heed, live and share Truth!
O Holy Spirit, Spring of Truth, let Truth flow in me!

Day 32 – A Story of Virtuous Discernment

Joe's heart was broken as his girlfriend ditched him for no apparent reason. He thought she was his soul mate for life – after all, they were friends since their sophomore year in high school. But they went to different colleges, he to Albany and she to UCLA. *The separation between them is what did it,* Joe mused.

Joe talked to an older brother in Christ, Ray, who listened to him and prayed with him. Ray asked, "Have you considered asking the Lord to send you His choice of a spouse for you? I know some folks enter into a time of fasting and prayer for a year, forty days, twenty-one days, seven days, or a particular day of the week. Do not be afraid to ask Him for the qualities you wish to have in your spouse but most of all *be* that spouse you are seeking. Then, honor her when He sends her to you." Joe did a weekly fast.

Two years later, Joe married Catherine, whom he met on Catholic Match.com. He learned that Catherine, too, had offered prayer and fasting – a 40 day fast— that God would send her a holy spouse.

Jesus: "My child, I reside in hearts that live in truth."

I: "Jesus, I trust Your answer to prayer if I stay pure!"

Day 33 – Virtue of Patience

St. Paul exhorts the Corinthians with, "Love is patient. Love is kind" (1 Corinthians 13:1). But, does patience always reflect loving-kindness? Not always. That is, if we are honest with ourselves. To constantly show loving-kindness towards God, one another, and ourselves, we ought to seek the Holy Spirit Himself, His seven gifts, and His nine fruit.

Patience flows from the seven gifts of the Holy Spirit given to us at our baptism. The gifts are as follows: *wisdom, understanding, counsel, knowledge, fortitude, piety, and fear of the Lord* (Isaiah 11:2-3).

Wisdom holds the key to right thinking, words, gestures, and actions in our daily interactions with God, neighbor, and self. *Understanding* enables souls to perceive God's ways and how He created each person uniquely, some to be the epitome of patience, and others to test our patience. *Counsel* allows the Holy Spirit to direct our souls to correct responses and action in every situation that causes ire or hurt, and to encourage other souls, too, in a holy direction.

Knowledge helps our souls understand what our God-given talents are to support the good of the other, and what our limitations are in serving others. *Fortitude* gives us the courage to suffer patiently in the walk of grace and truth, and win the race. *Piety* draws us more towards God to beg His patience and mercy upon us, and intercede for the gift of patience in loving Him and loving all His children. *Fear of the Lord* or *awe* allows us to see and experience God and heaven, not only in all His blessings, but especially in every trying moment – past, present, and future.

Patience, perhaps, is the key fruit of the Holy Spirit, that is, the guardian of all the nine fruits (yes including itself), which St. Paul lists as: *"love, joy, peace, patience, kindness, generosity, faithfulness, gentleness, and self-control"* (Galatians 5:22).

Love with patience protects, nourishes, and cherishes life until natural death. Its mantra is, "No human being is an inconvenience." Or, "I have time for you." *Joy with patience* counters sadness and lifts up the hearts of despairing souls. Its words of hope may sound like this, "God destined you for joy everlasting." Or, "You will receive a crown of joy for this transitory and earthly suffering!" *Peace with patience* minimizes discord and looks for peaceful resolutions even before a seed of conflict germinates. It asks, "How may I share with you what I have, neighbor?"

Patience with patience is essentially long-suffering that demands loving sacrifice of one's time, talent, and treasure, shared especially with one's family. Onlookers say to souls who embody *patience with patience*, "Your purgatory is happening here." *Kindness with patience* is constantly polite and courteous. It knows that the recipient of one's affection may not, at times, be worthy of such love but still offers mercy anyway. It believes that only consistent forgiveness, born from the Father's heart, can restore relationships and change hardness of heart. *Generosity with patience* gives without counting the cost and until it hurts the giver. It believes that its giving will multiply, and it provides basic needs of food, shelter, and clothing while supporting its beneficiaries' souls. It does not ask to be paid back.

Faithfulness with patience submits to God and one another and keeps such covenants sacred. It chooses God and says, "Yes" to chaste and holy relationships with all family and friends. *Gentleness with patience* accepts and returns love to God and one another through docility. The intended harsh word becomes a gentle question as a child would ask: "How are you feeling?" "What may I do to help?" "Whom do you serve?" If God or a person is sad or hurt, then the soul offers gentle consolation. If a person, whom God created, needs help, then the soul gently offers to assist. Gentleness towards others reflects a genuineness of true worship of God. *Self-control with patience* checks itself with prayers, penances, almsgiving, sacrifice, and mortifications, to overcome the "I" and eradicate irrational thoughts, words, and actions.

Come, Holy Spirit, come!   Annet O'Mara

Day 33 – Reflections on the Virtue of Patience

"Better is the end of a thing, than its beginning; better is a patient spirit than a lofty one. Do not let anger upset your spirit, for anger lodges in the bosom of a fool"
— Ecclesiastes 7:9.

"Patience is the companion of wisdom" — St. Augustine.

"Have patience with all things, but, first of all with yourself"
— St. Francis de Sales.

"Patience, prayer, and silence…this is what gives strength to the soul" — St. Faustina Kowalska.

"Fight all error, but do it with good humor, patience, kindness and love. Harshness will damage your own soul and spoil the best cause" — St. John Climcacus.

"Nothing great is ever achieved without much enduring"
— St. Catherine of Siena.

"It is with the smallest brushes that the artist paints the most exquisitely beautiful pictures" — St. Andre Bessette.

"Be gentle to all, but stern with yourself"
— St. Teresa of Avila.

Avalanche of Grace!

Day 33 – Prayer for the Virtue of Patience

Read God's Word: Genesis 18: 1-33

O Father, *Abba*, who waits for my daily return!
O Jesus, Savior, in Your cross, may I learn patience!
O Holy Spirit, Wisdom of God, teach me patience!

O Holy Trinity, in Your stream of humility, I ask to:
be patient with You, O God, in adversity;
be patient with myself when evils of life beset me;
be patient with others and intercede for them;
be patient lest my heart gives rent to anger;
be patient lest my anger damages even one soul;
be patient lest my folly destroys my own soul;
and, be patient in waiting on Your answer to prayers!

O Jesus, Your crown of life awaits the humble,
who with gentle patience, love God and neighbor
to the fullest!

O Father, forgive the paths I tread to reach You!
O Jesus, Patience of God, find in me real patience!
O Holy Spirit, I wait patiently for a new spring!

Day 33 – A Story of Virtuous Patience

Keisha had suffered from arthritis for many years. She went to a Marian conference for the opening healing Mass and adoration. No one knew what physical and emotional pain she suffered though pain was written on her face and comportment. "May I come tomorrow?" she asked. "I have not signed up." "Of course, you may," Diana, the organizer said.

Keisha came back the next day, and listened to the inspirational talks on faith, healing, and discipleship. She participated in praise and worship and the sacraments. "May I come again tomorrow?" she asked once more. Now, it was Jesus and Mary truly inviting her back for more.

During testimony time on Sunday, Keisha thanked and praised God, saying:

> I got up this morning with no pain whatsoever. My husband exclaimed, "I have not seen you smile continuously like this for twenty years!" I told him that Jesus healed me because I took

Our Blessed Mother into my heart and home. Patience is being open to God's daily invitations to enter into intimacy with Him. He is our hope.

Jesus: "My child, Your total faith in Me heals You."

I: "Jesus, help all my unbelief!"

Avalanche of Grace!

Day 34 – Virtue of Honor and Integrity

Wholeness next to godliness

The difference between God and the devil is the difference between simplicity and multiplicity. We human beings cannot hope to achieve simplicity, but we can achieve integrity and avoid multiplicity.

A favorite theme among 20th-century writers is the fundamental moral importance of personal integrity. The word they often use to describe this state is authenticity. A person should be himself, they insist, and not divide himself into incompatible parts: one for himself and another for the masses.

Because our unity of personality demands the integration of its parts, there is always the possibility that we can break up (dis-integrate) into discordant pieces. But what are these parts that must be integrated if the person is to be whole? There are many lines along which personality can be unified. There is the integrity between word and deed, friendship and fidelity, private life and public life, mind and body, head and heart. But the integrity that is perhaps most basic to a human being is the one that binds one's being to one's behavior, endowment to achievement, or giftedness to response.

Claiming our inheritance

God has given us our inheritance and an inclination toward our destiny. We are free to reject this inheritance because we do not think it is good enough. Thus, we may spend our life envying others whom we judge to be more talented, intelligent, attractive, and so on. Or we may decide not to make the effort of claiming our natural inheritance so as to fulfill our destiny. The great Christian existentialist Søren Kierkegaard distinguished these two dispositions, respectively, as the despair of weakness and the despair of defiance.

We need integrity to become who we are, so that we can complement God's gift to us with our gift to Him. Although we often lack integrity in ourselves, we are usually quick to recognize and denounce it in others. ... We detest phoniness, hypocrisy, duplicity, double-dealing, and disingenuousness. We admire integrity, though we know that it often comes at a high price.

Specialization and bureaucracy contribute heavily to the process of disintegration. Politics is another area that poses a formidable challenge to anyone who wants to retain his integrity. On the abortion issue, for example, one commonly hears about politicians who are privately opposed but publicly in favor of it. ...

(Excerpt from Donald DeMarco's "The Virtue of Integrity.")

Day 34 – Reflections on the Virtue of Honor and Integrity

"The honesty [integrity] of the upright guides them. The faithless are ruined by their duplicity" —Proverbs 11:3.

"Do not accept anything as the truth if it lacks love. And do not accept anything as love which lacks truth"
—St. Edith Stein.

"A person's rightful due is to be treated as an object of love, not as an object for use" —St. John Paul II.

"Take even bread with moderation lest a loaded stomach should make you weary of prayer"
—St. Bernard of Clairvaux.

"The greatest honor God can give a soul is not to give it too much but to ask much of it" —St. Therese of Lisieux.

"Now we must help each other get to heaven"
—Blessed Karl of Austria.

"Be sure that you preach by the way you live. If you do not, people will notice that you will say something, but live otherwise, and your words will bring only cynical laughter and a derisive shake of the head" —St. Charles Borromeo.

Avalanche of Grace!

Day 34 –Prayer for the Virtue of Honor and Integrity

Read God's Word: 2 Timothy 2: 1-26

O Father, in Mary, You gave us the highest honor!
O Jesus, Faithful One, help me stay loyal to You!
O Holy Spirit, like You, may I bless all without bias!

O Holy Trinity, help me to be whole in You, as I:
claim my eternal inheritance as a child of God;
honor God, parents, family, spouse, and neighbor;
give only that born in love and truth;
walk the talk, and not merely talk the talk;
cooperate with grace to fulfill my destiny;
share my talents and gifts for the good of all souls;
sincerely love the other with no duplicity;
and, show consistency in my private and public life.

O Jesus, renew me by Our Blessed Mother's heart!

O Father, Author of Truth, may I give You honor!
O Jesus, the Truth, may I heed, live and share truth!
O Holy Spirit, Spring of Truth, let truth flow in me!

Day 34 – A Story of Virtuous Honor and Integrity

Second Lieutenant Greg, 28, was serving his second tour in the Middle East when he got badly hurt.

The bombs had exploded in the building. Once outside, Greg counted and found one soldier missing. He went back in to get the soldier and got injured in the process. That's when he lost his hearing. For saving his friend's life, he was awarded the Purple Heart. As Greg recuperated, the chaplain gave him a copy of the *Magnificat* and so he began praying the Mass readings, studying the bible and the Church Fathers.

Raised in a non-denominational church, Greg was struck by John 6's *Real Presence* and the books of *Maccabees*. He asked his chaplain what he needed to do to receive Holy Communion. The chaplain shared the *Catholic Catechism* with him.

The following Easter, he was received into the church. Greg received the Sacred Heart for eternity. Back to a civilian life, Greg decided to work for the salvation of souls. "Ask much of me, Lord, for your greater glory," he said.

Jesus: *"My child, you are whole when you receive Me."*

I: *"Jesus, let my soul stay whole in You!"*

Day 35 – Virtue of Faithfulness

Faithfulness: responding out of faith

Being faithful: seeking, welcoming, being consistent and constant. Mary's life was a faith-filled response to the most varied situations. This response was made possible because she was deeply moved when she received God's messages, and meditated on them. Our Lord himself, when an enthusiastic woman burst out in words of praise for his Mother, pointed to the real reason why she deserved it: *Blessed rather are those who hear the word of God and keep it!* This is one of the most important lessons we can learn from Mary: faithfulness is not improvised; rather it is built up day after day. One cannot learn to be faithful spontaneous-ly. It is true that the virtue of faithfulness is a disposition that is born of a firm resolution to respond to the call we receive, and that prepares us to welcome God's plan for us. But this decision demands a "constant consistency" from each one.

The perseverance that fidelity requires has nothing to do with inertia or monotony. Our lives unfold in a continuous succession of impressions, thoughts and actions; our minds, wills and feelings are moving constantly from one object to another, and experience shows that it is impossible for human faculties to remain concentrated upon a single object for a long time. Therefore unity of life requires realizing that over and above any given event, we have the capacity to organize our own scale of values, meditating on events and evaluating them and thus sorting out the ones that are truly important, in order to be consistent with the course of life we have chosen. Otherwise we would only be able to concentrate on the experience of the moment, and end up in superficiality and inconsistency. As St. Paul says, *"All things are lawful for me," but not all things are helpful. "All things are lawful for me," but I will not be enslaved by anything.*

A Christian evaluates events in the light of faith; by this light we discover which are the truly important events, and receive the message they hold and make them a reference-point for our actions. A person who is faithful is guided by the genuine meaning of events in one's life, so that the truly important realities, such as God's love, our divine filiation, the certainty of our vocation, and Christ's nearness in the Sacraments, effectively guide our behavior and produce firm attitudes in us.

St. Josemaria said: "Only people who are inconstant and superficial change the object of their love from one day to the next." And, referring to the star that guided the Wise Men, he said: "If vocation comes first, if the star shines ahead to start us along the path of God's love, it is illogical that we should begin to doubt if it chances to disappear from view. It might happen at certain moments in our interior life—and we are nearly always to blame—that the star disappears, just as it did to the wise kings on their journey. We have already realized the divine splendor of our vocation, and we are convinced about its definitive character, but perhaps the dust we stir up as we walk—our miseries—forms an opaque cloud that cuts off the light from above."

Were something like this to happen to us, we need to remember the decisive moments in our life when we saw what God was asking of us and we made generous decisions to be faithful to him.

Thus, our memory has a key role to play in our fidelity, because it can evoke the *magnalia Dei,* the great things that God has done in our own lives. Our personal experience becomes a fount of dialogue with our Lord: it is one more spur to be consistent and faithful. St. Josemaria saw in the virtue of fidelity the effective result of the full commitment of human freedom that aspires to the highest gifts; it is a continual self-giving: a love, a generosity, a self-renunciation that lasts, and not merely the result of inertia. This can be seen in Mary's life, and in the history of the Chosen People: *Remember these things, O Jacob, and Israel, for you are my servant; I formed you, you are my servant; O Israel, you will not be forgotten by me. I have swept away your transgressions like a cloud, and your sins like mist; return to me, for I have redeemed you.* Remembering

God's goodness, in the world and in each person, moves us to be loyal.

(Excerpt from J.J. Marcos' "Learning to be Faithful.")

Avalanche of Grace!

Day 35 – Reflections on the Virtue of Faithfulness

"...regard us: as servants of Christ and stewards of the mysteries of God. Now it is of course required of stewards that they be found trustworthy" —1 Corinthians 4:1-2.

"God has not called me to be successful. He has called me to be faithful" —St. Teresa of Calcutta.

"This is the goodness ('bonum') of marriage: offspring, chaste fidelity and the unbreakable bond" —St. Augustine of Hippo.

"I will go to confession and communion often. I will keep holy the feast days. Jesus will be my best friend. I would rather die than commit a sin" —St. Dominic Savio.

"Faithfulness in little things is a big thing"
—St. John Chrysostom.

"Go often to rest your heart near the tabernacle; you will find there the necessary graces to go more surely along the path of fidelity" —St. Leonie Aviat.

"I die the king's faithful servant, but God's first"
—St. Thomas More.

Avalanche of Grace!

Day 35 – Prayer for the Virtue of Faithfulness

Read God's Word: Ezekiel 36: 1-38

O Father, You gather all back to Your land!
O Jesus, Faithful One, You righteously fight for me!
O Holy Spirit, You refresh my spirit daily!

O Holy Trinity, I need your aid to be faithful to:
You, God, for You have espoused me forever;
You, God, in whose holy name I was baptized;
You, God, in little things and in big things;
You, God, by avoiding sin and seeking confession;
You, God, in receiving Your Body worthily;
my call to adoration no matter my state in life;
my call to holiness no matter my state in life;
and, my call to charity no matter my state in life.

O Jesus, You are the Everlasting Bridegroom!
O Jesus, Your Church is the Ever Faithful Bride!

O Father, Your divine filiation brings me great joy!
O Jesus, Eternal Spouse, let me die for love of You!
O Holy Spirit, deep within, teach me fidelity!

Avalanche of Grace!

Day 35 – A Story of Virtuous Faithfulness

The young adult leader posed the question, "Have you ever put God second, maybe on a Sunday, and reaped its fruit?"

Lina, 32, offered, "Yes, I was faithful and would walk to church at least two miles each Sunday for Mass. One day it was pouring cats and dogs so I did not go to church. But I did have a blind date that night which did not go well. He seemed angry because I was not *that* type of woman, if you know what I mean."

"After dinner, the irate date was driving 55 miles per hour in a 30 mile zone. I prayed desperately that the Holy Spirit would intervene and He somehow did. This date ran a red light as a Jeep was making a left into our path. The front windshield of the sports car we were in shattered. We were not hurt but people in the Jeep were. I was fortunate that a friend driving by, who always stops at accidents, as she knows CPR, stopped to offer help. She gave me a ride home."

Lina said, "The lesson I learned was to love God above all and give God His due on the Sabbath – keep it holy. He will bless you. He saved me so I am totally indebted to him. Now, I try to get to daily Mass, too."

Jesus: "My child, faithfulness rests in My Heart."

I: "Jesus, in Your Heart, I stay close. Let me rest!"

Day 36 – Virtue of Accountability

The first instance required in spiritual accountability is truth. No one ever wants to be lied to or be led into a false narrative. We are bound to always seek the truth and embrace it *(CCC 2104)*. Whether we attempt to hold someone spiritually or morally accountable for their actions, our intentions must be directed towards Christ for the sake of their soul. This means we should first recognize the dignity of the human person. Holding someone spiritually or morally accountable involves a gradual but firm movement toward a conversion of heart. This is so the person in question does not feel threatened and understands the concerns brought to his attention.

…Before you decide the time has come to hold someone accountable, it is important you have prayerfully discerned this is the best time to initiate the process. Accountability is not dictatorial — it's an opportunity to engage in a direct conversation about someone's behavior and address it in a respectful and prayerful manner. …

…St. Padre Pio offers us a great reflection on spiritual and moral self-accountability: [Assuming that once we have repented, confessed and received absolution for our sins and experienced a true conversion of heart],

[a]ny mental picture of your life that focuses on past sins is a lie and this comes from the devil. Jesus loves you and has forgiven you your sins, so there is no room for having a downcast spirit. Whatever persuades you otherwise is truly a waste of time. It is also something that offends the heart of our very tender Lover. On the other hand, if the mental picture of your life consists in what you can be or could be, then it comes from God.

(Excerpt from Marlon De La Torre's *Is Holding Someone Accountable a Virtue?*.)

Day 36 – Reflections on the Virtue of Accountability

"So [then] each of us shall give an account of himself [to God]"
—Romans 14: 12.

"If you see your neighbor sinning take care not to dwell exclusively on his faults. Try to think of the many good things he has done. Many times when we do this, we come to the conclusion that our neighbor is a far better person than we are" —St. Basil the Great.

"A good conscience is a treasury of riches. Indeed – what greater riches can there be – or what can be sweeter than a good conscience" —St. Bernard Clairvaux.

"You cannot reap what you have not sown. How are we going to reap love in our community, if we only sow hate?"
—St. Oscar Romero.

"What have you to fear? Are you afraid of the divine craftsman who wants to perfect his masterpiece in this way?"
—St. Pio of Pietrelcina.

"We cannot have it both ways: if we are free we are responsible. If we are not responsible, we are not free"
—Blessed Fulton Sheen.

Avalanche of Grace!

Day 36 – Prayer for the Virtue of Accountability

Read God's Word: Matthew 12: 28-37

O Father God, thank You for giving me a free will!
O Jesus, I want to choose Your right path always!
O Holy Spirit, I want to revere Your Name forever!

O Holy Trinity, help me to be accountable for:
listening to Jesus and following His voice;
owning up to mistakes I make or have made;
repairing the damage caused by my sins;
and, for uttering words that are hurtful to souls.
Help me speak the truth that all may be set free.
Help me act in justice to serve the voiceless.
Help me give God, family, and country their due.

O Father, may I let You be God in all things!
O Jesus, help me to be ethically accountable to all!
O Holy Spirit, help me own up to my shortcomings!

O Father, Just Judge, I shall one day meet You!
O Jesus, Divine Mercy, I trust in Your merciful love!
O Holy Spirit, I ask for the grace of accountability!

Day 36 – A Story of Virtuous Accountability

Paulina, a city girl, came from a working class home and so knew what it was to wake up at the crack of dawn and work until her bones ached.

"You will work until 10 P.M. no matter what they tell you, for that is what you are paid for. If it means mopping up the place, then do it," Paulina told her son, Marco, when he took on his first job.

Paulina taught all her six children not to expect payment for any work done for family or the neighbors. "Refuse it for you are getting free apprenticeship in putting down a slab or building a porch. Your knowledge gained while working the job is invaluable." She taught them to refuse donations for serving as altar servers at funeral or wedding Masses. Paulina reasons with them –"Lectors do not get paid, why should you get paid for what you are obliged to do, to serve God and your church?"

It is no wonder that one of Paulina's children serves in the army and another on a Special Weapons And Tactics (SWAT) team in Los Angeles. The children were taught to serve without counting the cost, even that of their lives.

Jesus: "My child, You serve Me when you serve others."

I: "Let me serve and be accountable to You, Lord!"

Day 37 – Virtue of Docility

... 1) Docility means being easily taught by the Holy Spirit.
- "[Missionary] spirituality is expressed first of all by a life of complete docility to the Spirit. It commits us to being molded from within by the Spirit, so that we may become ever more like Christ" (St. John Paul II, *Redemptoris Missio*, 87).
- "Do not conform yourself to this age, but be transformed by the renewal of your mind, that you may discern what is the will of God, what is good and pleasing and perfect" (Rom 12:2).
- Docility is having a "What would Jesus Do?" bracelet on your soul!
  "A son cannot do anything on his own, but only what he sees his father doing" (John 5:19).
  "I do not seek my own will, but the will of the Father" (John 5:30).

2) Docility is the key to effective evangelization
- Ex. Francis McNutt's book on Healing, a man who had the gift of healing decided to go to a hospital and pray with each of the sick. To his dismay no one was getting healed, so he asked the Lord why. Response: "Did I ask you to go to the hospital and pray with all the sick?"
- We must always be attentive to the Spirit's direction in each situation. If we don't, we can end up wasting

a lot of time and effort on projects and approaches that are ineffective.

(Ex. Peter fishing all night and catching nothing, vs. the big catch under Jesus' direction)

3) Docility in spiritual conversations
- Docility means keeping one "ear" on the person and one "ear" on the Lord.
- Each person God created is unique, unique experiences in life, obstacles which block conversion. Docility puts us in a responsive mode, responding to the Holy Spirit who knows what each person needs.

Ex. Walking into a Room:–A docile person asks the Lord questions ("Who do you want me to talk to? What should I say to this person?") and listens in his heart for the leading of the Spirit. Maybe we need to give them a book, or they are hungry and need food, or we may just have to pray and listen. We can do this anywhere: during school, at Mass, in your family life, on mission.

If we're following the lead of the Spirit, we can evangelize with confidence in the Lord.

PRAYER: Come Holy Spirit, fill the hearts of your faithful and enkindle in us the fire of your love. ...

ACTION: ...[A]sk God about what He wants, each moment of the day.

(Excerpt from "Docility" in *Companions of the Cross*.)

Avalanche of Grace!

Day 37 – Reflections on the Virtue of Docility

"Accept whatever happens to you; in periods of humiliation be patient. For in fire gold is tested, and the chosen, in the crucible of humiliation" — Sirach 2: 4-5.

"However great a sinner may be, if he shows himself devout to Mary, he will never perish" — St. Hilary of Poitiers.

"Be more docile to the internal voice of God"
— St. Eugene de Mazenod.

"Never will anyone who says the rosary every day be led astray" — St. Louis de Montfort.

"Be who God meant you to be and you will set the world on fire" — St. Catherine of Siena.

"I am a piece of twisted iron. I entered the religious life to be twisted straight" — St. Aloysius of Gonzaga.

"All battles are first won or lost in the mind" — St. Joan.

"We must sow the seed, not hoard it" — St. Dominic Osma.

"The Holy Spirit leads us like a mother. He leads His child by the hand...like a sighted person leads a blind person"
— St. Jean Marie Vianney.

Avalanche of Grace!

Day 37 – Prayer for the Virtue of Docility

Read God's Word: Isaiah 6: 1-13

O Father, You choose the docile for Your work!
O Jesus, Lamb of God, led to slaughter!
O Holy Spirit, You prompt us to the Father's will!

Holy Trinity,
let me listen to Your voice, follow, and obey You.
Teach my heart how to love You today.
Direct my soul to whomever I ought
listen to, talk to, or counsel today.
I submit all the Holy Spirit's gifts
given to me for Your greater glory in my family,
parish, school, work-place, and nation.

I offer my mind, spirit and will to You.
Mold me and transform my thoughts, words,
and deeds that I may become more Christ-like.

O Father, let me hear Your voice, *Abba*, and love You.
O Jesus, I submit as You did to our *Abba*'s heart.
O Holy Spirit, teach me docility in executing Your will.

Day 37 – A Story of Virtuous Docility

Docility of spirit germinates future saints. St. Frances Cabrini wanted to go east to China but the Pope sent her west to the United States to work among the poor. Likewise, in 1950, Fr. Ralph Beiting's bishop sent him to Berea, Central Kentucky.

God provided Fr. Beiting with his first volunteers from among his dad, mom, and siblings who went down to help him build his rectory and chapel. The very neighbor who, at first, wanted him thrown out of the town, later spoke up for him, respectfully calling him "Father," and saying that he had come to believe he was "the only minister in town who's worth a d*&n" (Salatino 73). He later sold his own home to Fr. Beiting.

Fr. Beiting lived out his oft quoted phrase, "Have you asked God what He wants to do in your life?" During holy hours before the Blessed Sacrament, he would ask Jesus for guidance to help more folks with basic needs. Jesus' provision always came through and gave Fr. Beiting a sense of peace.

Jesus: "My child, ask me and I will answer you."

I: "Who will You send me to today, Jesus? Come, Holy Spirit, come! Let me listen and follow Your leading."

Avalanche of Grace!

Day 38 – Virtue of Simplicity

…The word *simplicity* has a few different meanings, and it seems that St. Vincent [de Paul] embraced three of them. First, simplicity means freedom from complexity or division into parts; second, the absence of luxury or ornament; and third, freedom from deceit or guile. Each of these meanings is important if we are to understand why St. Vincent esteemed simplicity so highly,…

1. Simplicity as having a single aim or purpose
"You shall love the Lord your God with all your heart, and with all your soul, and with all your mind" (Matt. 22:37).

St. Vincent wanted his priests and nuns to be simple in the sense that they did everything out of love of God, and not for other reasons. He did not want them to do things to impress their superior or out of human respect. He wanted them to be single-minded in their intentions and in their pursuit of God's will. Too often, our intentions are not pure, and we act according to our own will, instead of God's. This hinders us from flying to God in our thoughts, in our prayers, and in our hearts throughout the day. It also prevents God from working in us the way He could if we abandoned ourselves to His will.

2. Simplicity in material possessions

"When Jesus heard this, he said to him, 'There is still one thing lacking. Sell all that you own and distribute the money to the poor, and you will have treasure in heaven" (Lk 18:22).

St. Vincent asked his priests not to have any superfluous furniture, pictures or books in their rooms, and to avoid owning any vain or useless things. He knew that possessions bring attachment, and attachments hinder us from living for God in complete freedom. After all, St. Vincent wanted to imitate Christ in everything, and it was He who was born in a stable and had "no place to lay his head." (Lk 9:58) How can we live this kind of simplicity in our lives? Are there unnecessary purchases we could sacrifice, and instead give that money to the poor? Are there items in our homes that we do not use that could be donated to someone who could use them? As Christians, it is important to reflect often upon what we are doing for our less fortunate brothers and sisters – in our neighborhood, in our country, and around the world. If we want to imitate Christ the way St. Vincent did, we must be willing to go without in order to help those who are in need.

3. Simplicity as sincerity

"Here is a true Israelite, in whom there is no guile or deceit" (Jn 1:47).

Above all, simplicity for St. Vincent was sincerity in one's words and actions. He tried to always say things as they truly were, and to avoid any duplicity or deceit. He taught his followers, "The heart must not think one thing, while the mouth says another." He said that God speaks to the simple, and that simplicity is the spirit of Jesus. He wanted his communities to practice this virtue because the world is filled with so much duplicity. Of the three, this may be the most important form of simplicity for us to practice today.

We live in a society where it is considered normal to present an image of ourselves that is not authentic. Just as in St. Vincent's day, this is an obstacle for evangelization and service to the poor. If people sense any inauthenticity in us, then they know we cannot be trusted, and our message or service to them will be empty. On the other hand, if we have the courage and humility to be seen as we truly are, to speak the truth in love, and to do everything with authenticity as our guide, then we will be effective in sharing the gospel and in helping the poor, the way St. Vincent De Paul was. …

(Excerpt from Sarah Mett's "The Simplicity of Saint Vincent de Paul.")

Avalanche of Grace!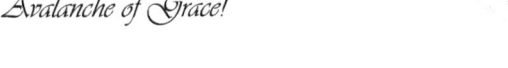

Day 38 – Reflections on the Virtue of Simplicity

"The law of the LORD is perfect, refreshing the soul. The decree of the LORD is trustworthy, giving wisdom to the simple" —Psalm 19:8.

"In everything, love simplicity" —St. Francis de Sales.

"Be humble, be simple, and bring joy to others" —St. Madeleine Sophie Barat.

"All my work began with a simple Hail Mary for Our Lady's help" —St. John Bosco.

"Remain humble, remain simple. The more you are so, the more good you will do" —St. Jean Marie Vianney.

"Holiness is not the luxury of the few. It is the simple duty for you and me" —St. Teresa of Calcutta.

"One earns Paradise with one's daily tasks" —St. Gianna Beretta Molla.

"It is a kingly act to assist the fallen" —St. Teresa of Calcutta.

"Remember that nothing is too small in God's eyes. Do all that you do with love" —St. Therese of Lisieux.

Avalanche of Grace!

Day 38 – Prayer for the Virtue of Simplicity

Read God's Word: Luke 2: 1-19

O Father, sublime Lord of the simple!
O Jesus, Your first adoration began in a stable!
O Holy Spirit, simple fire whose blaze catches on!

Simply simple and selfless, Holy Trinity:
let my housing, décor, and garb be all for You;
let me smell, taste, feel, see, and hear through You;
let my plans, intentions, and motivations be in You;
and, let my failures and successes be offered to You.

In the Name of Jesus, I ask You, O Father, to:
take my pretentious home, furnishings, and outfits;
take my complex thoughts and inauthentic ways;
take my convoluted plans, intentions, and motivations;
and, take my narcissistic failures and successes.

Father, I am willing to simply be Your child.
Jesus, I am willing to simply love like You.
Holy Spirit, I am willing to let You set me on fire.

Avalanche of Grace!

Day 38 – A Story of Virtuous Simplicity

"They do not know *others'* wants to want. They are very resilient. Sub-flooring is what they need so that they will not find themselves hugging the earth below them in the middle of the night. Be attuned to smells that are different from what you are used to." The Father Beiting Appalachian Mission Center (FBAMC) coordinator told us that laminated vinyl was not even within range of vision for these poor people. After completing a job, when a volunteer asked the homeowner if she could have anything she liked, what it would be, she said, "Perhaps, Vaseline for my feet."

As I drove the screws into the first board, I whispered, "St. Joseph, pray for us." Joseph, a carpenter, probably felt at a loss that Jesus could not be born in a home that he had made. He and Mary were resilient and silent about Jesus' stable. He managed to clean out a manger and throw in some hay to keep baby Jesus warm. Joseph made it work. Myrrh and dung filled the air, ready for royalty and peasantry.

I had expected dung fumes outside and inside the trailer. Outside, my lungs filled with green crested hills, but inside I breathed cigarette fumes. Humbled.

Jesus: *"My child, I am all you'll ever need. I am simple."*

I: *"I need only You. Keep me simple of heart."*

Day 39 – Virtue of Humility

...Humility is freeing and makes you content only believing the truth of who you are in the mind of God.

From the desire of being loved, deliver me Jesus:
Do you want to be loved? Of course you do! This is a natural desire and is central to your human nature. You were made to give and receive love. So why would you want to be freed from the desire of being loved? The answer requires a very subtle distinction.

Love is not something that you can demand or expect. Love, if it is authentic, must be freely given and freely received. Therefore, it is good to desire authentic love, given freely and in a selfless way. However, the "desire" for this form of love is not a selfish desire. It is not a desire that leads you to say, "I *want* your love because I *need* to be loved by you." Rather, it is a desire that leads you to say, "If you freely choose to offer your love to me...thank you! I am most humbled and grateful." Authentic Christian love cannot be demanded, expected or required of another person. Therefore, when you pray to be delivered from the "desire" of being loved, you are praying to be freed from a desire for selfish love. Interestingly, if you have a selfish desire for the love of another, it can never be fulfilled. Selfishness simply cannot satisfy us. The only authentic way to enjoy the love of another is to first be purified of the desire for that love.

(Excerpt from John Paul Thomas' *The Path to Holiness: Becoming a Living Sacrifice of Love*.)

Day 39 – Reflections on the Virtue of Humility

"Who among you is wise and understanding? Let him show his works by a good life in the humility that comes from wisdom" — James 3:13.

"Humility, humility, and humility. Satan always trembles before humble souls" — St. Pio of Pietrelcina.

"Complete trust in God. That is what holy humility is" — St. Porphyrios.

"If you are humble, nothing will touch you, neither praise nor disgrace, because you know what you are" — St. Teresa of Calcutta.

"The truly humble reject all praise for themselves and refer it all to God" — St. Francis de Sales.

"If you elevate yourself, God distances Himself from you. If you humble yourself, He leans towards you" — St. Augustine of Hippo.

"How could I bear a crown of gold when my Lord bears a crown of thorns? And bears it for me!" — St. Elizabeth of Hungary.

Avalanche of Grace!

Day 39 – Prayer for the Virtue of Humility

Read God's Word: 1 Peter 5: 5-11

O Father, in humility, You gave me another chance!
O Jesus, Son of God and Man, who died for me!
O Holy Spirit, Father's and Son's fruit of humility!

O Trinity, I ask for the grace of humility to:
be thankful when I am not loved or respected;
credit all praise received to God's greater glory;
lay down my life for others and not for any gain;
count the blessings received, not the cost, in serving;
seek wisdom before every uttered word;
praise God for His work of salvation in me;
and, praise others for their giftedness and talents!

O Jesus, lean towards me with Your crown of thorns
when I am tempted to seek a crown of gold.

O Father, God of the Humble, I choose You today!
O Jesus, teach me to grow in humility!
O Holy Spirit, I ask for humility to grow in me!

Day 39 – A Story of Virtuous Humility

"We cannot hire you," said the director of HR. He was a person of color.

"But I am on a work visa and I was already hired by the chair of the Philosophy department."

"Why should we hire you when there are thousands of citizens wanting this job?"

Those thousands did not apply and are not here, Jane thought. Another case of "no room in the inn," she felt. Jane was not going to fight this so she prayed a rosary for the HR director on her way home and all his Caucasian women co-workers who were stunned by his outright racism, but dared not vocalize their dissent. Jane accepted another job, not quite up her alley, but it paid the bills.

At the local shrine, Jane listened to the band play and sing, "All Are Welcome," knowing that in the Catholic Church, *all* are daughters and sons of God, the Father, and have their rightful citizenship in heaven. Jane prayed in her heart. *O Gentle St. Anthony, teach me humility and gentleness towards all. There is hope. After all, St. Anthony, born in Lisbon, became St. Anthony of Padua. Italy found and gained whom Portugal nurtured.*

Jesus: "My child, pray for those who do you wrong."

I: "Jesus, I want to pray unceasingly for their souls."

Day 40 – Virtue of Trust

Entrusting yourself to God first requires that you embrace the fundamental truth that *you can do nothing good without God*. Period. Understanding this fact is essential to the virtue of trust. God, and God alone, is the source of all goodness in life. Without Him, you are left to your sins and to a life of misery. It is sometimes hard to believe that you are powerless to do anything good without the grace of God. However, the truth is that no gift, talent or quality you have is sufficient to make it on your own and to produce good fruit in your life. You are powerless by your own effort to walk down the path of holiness. …

Faith can be described as both *passive* [and] *active*. First, a "passive faith" is sufficient to arrive at the *belief* that God is the one and only source of all goodness in your life. …Once you believe that God is the only source of all goodness in your life, you must then enter into an "active faith" in God. Having an "active" faith means that you allow your belief, present in your intellect, to move also into your will and ultimately your desires. In other words, you must allow what you have come to believe to *change you*. You must make a free choice to let God take over your life and produce good fruit in it.

...The result of *believing* in God and *entrusting* yourself to Him is the glorious transformation of your soul. ...

(Excerpts from John Paul Thomas' *The Path to Holiness: Becoming a Living Sacrifice of Love.*)

Avalanche of Grace!

Day 40 – Reflections on the Virtue of Trust

"When I am afraid, in You I place my trust...I praise the word of God; I trust in God, I do not fear" —Psalm 56: 4-5.

"No one was ever lost because his sin was too great, but because his trust was too small" —St. Francis Xavier Seelos.

"I place my trust in God, my creator, in all things; I love Him with all my heart" —St. Joan of Arc.

"Order your soul: reduce your wants; live in charity; associate in Christian community; obey the laws; trust in providence" —St. Augustine of Hippo.

"I trust in God and wish nothing else but His will" —St. Zygmunt Felinski.

"He who trusts himself is lost. He who trusts in God can do all things" —St. Alphonsus Liguori.

"Entrust everything to Jesus in the Blessed Sacrament and to Mary Help of Christians and you will see what miracles are" —St. John Bosco.

"Courage, courage, trust in God who helps you in all things" —St. Mary MacKillop.

Avalanche of Grace!

Day 40 – Prayer for the Virtue of Trust

Read God's Word: Isaiah 43: 1-14

O Father, I trust in You, the Father Almighty!
O Jesus, I trust in You, the only Son of our Lord!
O Holy Spirit, I trust in You, the Giver of Life!

O Holy Trinity, I ask for an outpouring of trust to:
thank and praise You for all graces yet to come;
stay courageous and trust in You in all trials;
know You will guide and protect me from all evil;
believe in Your power to heal me when in pain;
trust I am in Your Heart, now and forever;
overcome and do all things for Your greater glory;
and, desire only Your holiness and will for me.

O Jesus, I entrust my will, intentions, intellect, words, and actions to Your Heart. Purify me!

O Father, God of Trust, I trust in You!
O Jesus, Heart of Trust, let my heart trust others!
O Holy Spirit, Spirit of Trust, renew trust within me!

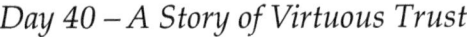

Day 40 – A Story of Virtuous Trust

1942. Maria prayed earnestly to God, "If he ever comes home, I will have as many children as You desire for Your kingdom." Her husband, Andre, had been declared MIA (Missing in Action) in France.

In mid 1945, Andre shows up at the very threshold he had brought Maria over just before he left for the war. Little did Maria know that Andre had promised God something, too. "Dear God, I will do whatever Maria wants of me if You will only take me home to her side."

They had fourteen children and three generations later, there are close to seventy in their clan. They placed their trust in God that they would see each other again and have children like olives around their table. Andre rejoiced in changing diapers, cleaning the house, and working in the factory to feed their children.

Both Andre and Maria knew that trusting God meant lovingly keeping their vows to each other and to God, and letting Him gift them with as many children as He chose. Since then, they have watched their children carve out their own stories of trust in God.

Jesus: "My child, I will fulfill Your desires. Trust in Me."

I: "Jesus, help my unbelief, Lord of hope and miracles."

Day 41– Virtue of Forgetting the Past

The operations of the soul in divine union are from the Holy Spirit; the actions of such souls are only those that are seemly and reasonable. God's Spirit teaches them what they ought to know and causes them to be ignorant of what they ought not to know, to remember what they have to remember, and to forget what they should forget. It makes them love what they have to love, and not to love what does not pertain to God. The first motions of the faculties of such souls are divine, and we must not wonder at this because they are being transformed in the Divine Being.

The spiritual person needs habitually to practice caution. Everything that he hears, sees, smells, tastes, or touches, he must be careful not to store up or collect in his memory, but he must allow himself to forget them immediately. This he must accomplish, if need be, with the same effectiveness as that which others use to remember them. As a result no knowledge or image of them remains in his memory.

Imperfections meet the soul at every step if it sets its memory on what it has heard, seen, touched, smelled, or tasted. If it does, some sort of feeling has to cling to it, whether pain, fear, hatred, vain hope, or vain enjoyment. At the least, these are imperfections, and at times, they are downright sins. Subtly, they leave much impurity in the soul, even though the reflections and knowledge have relation to God.

These things engender desire within the soul, for they arise naturally from knowledge and reflections; if one merely wishes to have knowledge and reflections, even that is a desire. Many occasions of judging others will also come, since in using its memory, the soul cannot fail to discover the good and the bad in others. In such a case what is evil often seems good, and what is good, evil. There is no one who can completely free himself from all these kinds of evil, except by blinding the memory and leading it into darkness in regards to all these things.

Let the soul, then, remain "enclosed," without anxieties and troubles; and the One who entered in physical form to his disciples when the doors were shut and gave them peace, though they neither thought this was possible nor knew how it was possible, will enter spiritually into the soul without its knowing how he does so, when the doors of its faculties – memory, understanding, and will – are enclosed against all things. He will fill them with peace coming down on the soul, as the prophet says, like a river, taking it from all the misgivings, suspicions, disturbances, and darkness that caused it to fear…

(Excerpts from St. John of the Cross' *Ascent of Mount Carmel*.)

Day 41 – Reflections on the Virtue of Forgetting the Past

"For if you do not forgive others, neither will your Father forgive your transgressions" —Matthew 6: 15.

"Prayer is forgetting earthly things, an ascent to Heaven. Through prayer we flee to God" —St. Nektarios.

"I lost myself. Forgot myself. I lay my face against my Beloved's face. Everything fell away and I left myself behind, abandoning my cares among the lilies, forgotten"
—St. John of the Cross.

"Forgiveness is above all a personal choice, a decision of the heart to go against natural instinct..." —St. John Paul II.

"You have not only my forgiveness, but my thanks"
—Blessed Miguel Pro.

"The memory of insults is the residue of anger"
—St. John Climacus.

"No one heals himself by wounding another" —St. Ambrose.

"After Christ's example, I forgive my persecutors. I do not hate them. I ask God to have pity on all, and I hope my blood will fall on my fellow men as a fruitful rain" —St. Paul Miki.

Avalanche of Grace!

Day 41 – Prayer for the Virtue of Forgetting the Past

Read God's Word: 1 Samuel 24: 9-23

O Father, God, who remembers not past sins!
O Jesus, Savior, who has redeemed all!
O Holy Spirit, who heals all our memories of hurt!

O Father, I plead for Your forgiveness and I repent, as:
in You, I rejoice gratefully for all the trials You sent me;
in You, I let go of all memories of hurt;
in You, I cease wounding You and others;
in You, I forgive my persecutors and pray for them;
in You, I let healthy thought seeds take root in me;
in You, I forget my sins, and especially, everyone else's;
and, in Your Heart, I place my heart. Heal my pain.

O Jesus, knit my heart to Your Heart
filled with love and mercy!
I want to radiate Your forgiveness!

O Father, God, who forgets my past, I hope in You!
O Jesus, Savior, save me from memories of hurt!
O Holy Spirit, Healer, heal all whom I have hurt!

Day 41 – A Story of Virtuous Forgetting of the Past

Parents wound. Siblings hurt. Families rage. Neighbors rile over fences. Communities fight. Tribes rant, strike, and kill. Nations go to war.

At her first young adult conference, Alice offered her story: "I came to the United States at the age of seven. The two major tribes on our island went to war over some disagreement of land rights. We fled the massacre. Overnight we were displaced and dispossessed of our land – refugees. My parents were disenfranchised. They had to begin anew in the US. My parents share this memory with us so that we can handle conflicts better. They say, 'Do not hold a grudge against anyone. Be at peace at all times with everyone and *share in love.*'"

Parents heal by showing the way to love. Siblings pass down clothes to younger ones. Families break bread together. Neighbors mow each other's lawn. Communities build towns and grow. Tribes share wisdom. Nations send timely medical aid and food to other nations. *To forget is to let God restore unity.*

Jesus: "My child, remember not your past or others' if you wish to enjoy perfect communion in Me eternally."

I: "Jesus, be the center of all my thoughts and affections and grace me with the gift of forgetting others' faults."

Day 42 – Virtue of True Beauty

God is true beauty and beautiful truth. What does this mean? God, the Father, is the authentic root of love and beauty. God, the Son, Jesus Christ, is the once-died-now-living shoot of love and beauty, springing forth from that root. And God, the Holy Spirit, is the Promise of the Father, the fruit of love and beauty.

All souls are created in God's image. That means, true beauty resides in all souls that live in the state of grace. When we have hurt the Father's heart by not loving Him above all and our neighbors as ourselves, we reject His true beauty for something false.

A false beauty might smack of a soul's turning inward to a total obsession with the self, or outward towards movie stars, musicians, or sports figures. Or, it might look like a turning towards something to gratify the senses or get a high, like an addiction to drugs, alcohol, sex, or pornography. Yet more, false beauty could take the semblance of a soul's craving for wealth, prestige, influence, and power, which necessarily means stepping over others to grab more than that which is fair and just.

Love for God and others takes a back-seat when false beauty replaces true beauty. Or, at least, until the soul realizes what is eating at his or her heart and takes the step to say, "Alas, I am completely lost. My soul, once pure, innocent, and beautiful is now soiled. Lest I die in this state, I must get up and go back to my Father's house!"

The Father waits for every single soul's return to His House. He waits to restore their purity, innocence, and beauty. He waits in love. He is faithful, even when souls are unfaithful to Him and leave His bosom.

The Father's objective standards for beauty never change, no matter how far or close souls are to Him. He *first* loved them. He created souls and knit them artfully in their mothers' wombs so that they could know, love, and serve Him in this life and the life after.

His beloved Son, Jesus Christ, offers a living taste of the Father's love even as souls journey back home. Jesus, the Son of God, now come in flesh as the Son of Mary, awakens one's soul's longing and desire for the Father. *If God can humble Himself to come as a baby, I can be humble to be found by Him and to ask for forgiveness of my sins.* Jesus' exalting of the woman who washes His feet with her tears pierces another soul to be a better child of the Father. *Jesus, You endured criticism. Save me from my detractors.*

Jesus' nails, Jesus' crown of thorns and Jesus being stripped of His garments instills remorse, repentance, and reparation in yet another soul. *How many nails have I driven into You, Lord? By my sins, how many crowns of thorns have I woven for You? How have I allowed myself to be stripped of the dignity of true beauty when I have done shameful things?* In the despairing soul, Jesus' empty tomb gives hope a chance to flourish. *You are alive, Jesus! I need Your Holy Spirit, who raised You from the dead, to resurrect my soul.*

The waiting Father runs, receives, and embraces lost souls. Lavishly, with His blessings and favor, He touches wounds and heals. The souls receive the Promise of the Father, the Helper, in a new way to bear the ambrosial fruit of *pulchra gaudium* (*Latin* for "beautiful joy"). And, the joy of heaven when souls are restored to their authentic beauty cannot be contained. God's true beauty overflows in such souls, and they will want to share this real beauty with all of the Father's children.

Annet O'Mara

Day 42 – Reflections on the Virtue of True Beauty

"How beautiful upon the mountains – are the feet of the one bringing good news, announcing peace…" — Isaiah 52:7.

"Since love grows within you, so beauty grows. Love is the beauty of the soul" — St. Augustine of Hippo.

"This world in which we live needs beauty in order that we may not sink in despair" — St. John Paul II.

"Do something beautiful for God" — St. Teresa of Calcutta.

"The tree that is beside running water is fresher and gives more fruit" — St. Teresa of Avila.

"All the darkness of the world cannot extinguish the light of a single candle" — St. Francis of Assisi.

"As you seek a virtuous spouse, it is fitting that you should be the same" — St. Bernardine of Siena.

"Christ made my soul beautiful with the jewels of grace and virtue. I belong to Him whom the angels serve"
— St. Agnes of Rome.

Avalanche of Grace!

Day 42 – Prayer for the Virtue of True Beauty

Read God's Word: 2 Corinthians 3: 7-18

O Father, God of All Beauty, You are beautiful!
O Jesus, Beauty blossomed in Your passion and death!
O Holy Spirit, Your wings hover over the Eucharist!

O Holy Trinity, You teach me openness to inner beauty:
as sunsets splash rose, pink, peach and lavender;
as loons, wood thrushes, and nightingales croon;
as magnolias, dogwoods, and yarrows pure out;
as red apples, maples, and oaks bleed – dying.

Of outer beauty, O Trinity, help me be vigilant:
as cow parsnips and poison sumac
blister their brushers;
and, giant hogweeds scar and blind their beholders.

O Jesus, I accept the soft wounds of Your True Beauty.

O Father of Infinite Beauty, break my finite tastes!
O Jesus, may I reflect truly on Your True Beauty!
O Holy Spirit, hid in Your wings, I seek True Beauty!

Day 42 – A Story of Virtuous True Beauty

"Shards of a champagne glass – this is how I felt at my lowest point," said Laurie. Failing several courses at Bresell University, Laurie was kicked out of the volleyball team for which she was captain. Things worsened as she got wounded by a few guy friends, leading her into despair. But the campus minister, Mary, was there for Laurie. Kneeling by her side in the little chapel, Mary began to gently guide Laurie into the Father's arms.

She said to Laurie, "Your Father loves you. You are precious in His sight. He gave His Son, Jesus, who died for you so that your soul may become as beautiful as He who loves you. Will you give Him a chance to show You what true beauty is?"

Laurie gave her life to Jesus, her True Beauty, that day. Her gentle Savior led her down a path she never would have imagined for her life. In time, Laurie became a campus minister and also coached volleyball for two years. Later, she consecrated her whole life to her one true love, Jesus. As a religious sister, she now helps single moms and babies. Truly beautiful.

Jesus: "My child, may I take you down the path of Beauty? I have you in my heart."

I: "Jesus, only if You walk with me and hold my heart."

Avalanche of Grace!

Day 43 – Virtue of Holiness

"All Christians in any state or walk of life are called to the fullness of Christian life and to the perfection of charity."[65] All are called to holiness: "Be perfect, as your heavenly Father is perfect."[66]

> In order to reach this perfection the faithful should use the strength dealt out to them by Christ's gift, so that ... doing the will of the Father in everything, they may wholeheartedly devote themselves to the glory of God and to the service of their neighbor. Thus the holiness of the People of God will grow in fruitful abundance, as is clearly shown in the history of the Church through the lives of so many saints.[67]

Spiritual progress tends toward ever more intimate union with Christ. This union is called "mystical" because it participates in the mystery of Christ through the sacraments–"the holy mysteries"–and, in him, in the mystery of the Holy Trinity. God calls us all to this intimate union with him, even if the special graces or extraordinary signs of this mystical life are granted only to some for the sake of manifesting the gratuitous gift given to all.

(Catechism of the Catholic Church 2013-2014)

Day 43 – Reflections on the Virtue of Holiness

"Therefore, gird up the loins of your mind, — live soberly, and set your hopes completely on the grace to be brought to you at the revelation of Jesus Christ. Like obedient children, do not act in compliance with the desires of your former ignorance — but, as he who called you is holy, be holy yourselves in every aspect of your conduct, for it is written, "Be holy because I [am] holy" —1 Peter 1:14-16.

"Holiness consists in one thing: to do God's will, as He wills it because He wills it" —St. Katharine Drexel.

"I want you to have a new concept of holiness. You've got to be holy where you are: washing dishes, at the office, at school. Wherever you are, you can be holy there" —Mother Angelica.

"You cannot be half a saint; you must be a whole saint or no saint at all" —St. Therese of Lisieux.

"Jesus is my great friend, and the Eucharist my highway to heaven" —Carlos Acutis, Servant of God.

"The higher we go, the better we shall hear the voice of Christ" —St. Pier Giorgio Frassati.

"When we pray, the voice of our hearts must be heard more than the proceedings from the mouth" —St. Bonaventure.

Avalanche of Grace!

Day 43 – Prayer for the Virtue of Holiness

Read God's Word: Philippians 2: 1-18

O Father, Holy are You, Lord God of Hosts!
O Jesus, Holy in emptying yourself on the cross!
O Holy Spirit, Holy is Your first Name!

Holy Trinity, I seek to be set apart to be holy:
I want to be forever in the Presence of the Father;
I want to strive for Jesus' holiness via *kenosis**;
I want to become more holy in the Holy Spirit;
I want to hear Your voice and follow Your will;
I want to know what I must renounce to be holy;
I want to live out my gift to be holy where I am;
I want to share holiness with all God's children;
and, I want You alone as my Lord, King and Savior.

O Father, increase Your holiness and charity in me!
O Jesus, may I arise from prayer to live as You did!
O Holy Spirit, I desire to do Your holy will for all!

kenosis* Greek – Jesus' self-emptying of His will in obedience to His Father.

Day 43 – A Story of Virtuous Holiness

Alicia explained how things got freaky in the house. Yes, she sprinkled holy water from time to time, but she still felt under attack as she tried to say *Hail Marys* when she could not sleep.

Tim, a prayer group leader, asked, "Have you been involved with Ouija boards, fortune-telling or crystal balls? "Yes, all of the above, but I was young," Alicia said. "Have you confessed this dependence on false spirits?" "No, but I have gone many times to confession. I did not think I needed to confess these," Alicia explained. Tim counseled Alicia saying, "Repent and confess these in the Sacrament of Reconciliation as soon as possible. Aim in your heart to serve only Jesus from now on. Do you wish to be set free?"

"Yes, I truly wish to be set free – once and for all!" Alicia said.

Tim said, "Then, please pray with me, 'Jesus, thank you for dying for me. I want to be set free and healed. In the name of Jesus Christ, Son of God and Son of Man, I renounce all forms of the occult and choose to serve You alone, Jesus — Faithful and True.'"

Jesus completely set Alicia free.

Jesus: "My little one, you are my sheep. Follow Me."

I: "I wish to follow only You, Jesus — all of me for You."

Day 44 – Virtue of Joy

...In common usage, "joy" and "happiness" could very well be seen as synonyms. One could say, "I was overjoyed at his coming," or "I was happy when he came," and mean the same thing. However, the words have two distinct meanings and applications. Even a casual listener would distinguish between "rejoice" and "be happy." Joy suggests a more complete, ecstatic, consuming passion than mere happiness. In short, "happiness" can be described as an emotion, while "joy" is more properly related to a *state of one's being.*

By definition, happiness is a response to *happen*stance, contentment, good luck, prosperity, or good fortune. Happiness is also a reaction to pleasure; one can be happy when eating ice cream, reading a good book, receiving a promotion at work, or experiencing anything pleasurable. The antonym of happiness is "sadness." The most elucidating definition of happiness, however, is this: an emotion experienced when in a state of well-being. Emotions are generally natural responses to outside influences that we do not control or will. That means that a rich or powerful man might be happy, but not necessarily joyful. Having sufficient material goods, as philosophers and moral theologians from Aristotle onward have pointed out, is not enough to satisfy the infinite longings of the human heart. Happiness is easily taken away when the "state of well-being" ceases; in times of hardship, trial, or need, happiness seems elusive. Something more satisfying is needed than the mere pleasure or contentment associated with happiness.

Joy, in contrast, is defined as an intense and especially ecstatic or exultant happiness or the expression of such feelings. The antonym of joy is "sorrow." "Enjoying" (related to happiness) is not the same thing as "rejoicing." Joy has several deeper meanings than happiness, which are further clarified in Holy Scriptures. In the Bible, joy can mean:

1. The response of the soul to a great and wonderful discovery, such as truth or communion with God.

#8226 Luke 1:44 — For as soon as I heard the sound of your greeting, the child in my womb leaped for joy.

#8226 Luke 19:6 — (Zacchaeus meets Christ) And he made haste and came down; and received Him with joy.

#8226 Luke 15:7 — I say to you, that even so there shall be joy in heaven upon one sinner that doth penance, more than upon ninety-nine just who need not penance.

2. A personal fullness or sense of completeness in one's entire life.

#8226 John 15:11 — These things I have spoken to you, that My joy may be in you, and your joy may be filled. (cf. also Jn 17:13)

3. A deep peace which comes from the indwelling of the Holy Spirit within a person, and lasts despite hardship.

#8226 John 16:22 — So also you now indeed have sorrow; but I will see you again, and your heart shall rejoice; and your joy no man shall take from you.

#8226 Romans 15:13 — Now the God of hope fill you with all joy and peace in believing; that you may abound in hope, and in the power of the Holy Ghost.

#8226 2 Corinthians 8:2 — That in much experience of tribulation, they have had abundance of joy; and their very deep poverty hath abounded unto the riches of their simplicity.

#8226 Galatians 5:22 — But the fruit of the Spirit is, charity, joy, peace, patience, benignity, goodness….

4. The fruit of faith, hope, and love.

#8226 Hebrews 10:34 — For you both had compassion on them that were in bands, and took with joy the being stripped of your own goods, knowing that you have a better and a lasting substance.

Even if these verses are translated in some editions with the word "happiness" instead of "joy," the deeper meaning is clear; these situations are not related to prosperity or good luck but true goodness that brings lasting peace.

"Joy" can also refer to the cause of joy in another. For example, St. Paul repeatedly refers to fellow Christians as his "joy" in a manner similar to a parent who refers to his child as "his pride and joy."

The Catechism also discusses the nature of joy and happiness. Paragraph 1723 teaches us "that true happiness is not found in riches or well-being, in human fame or power, or any human achievement...or indeed in any creature, but in God alone, the source of every good and of all love." In other words, temporal happiness is not enough to satisfy us; we long for the "joy of the Lord" (*CCC 1720*). Recognizing that God is our Creator and that we rely totally on Him is a "source of wisdom and freedom, of joy and confidence" (*CCC 301*). ...

(Excerpt from Elizabeth Hruska's' "The Difference between Joy And Happiness.")

Day 44 – Reflections on the Virtue of Joy

"Consider it all joy, my brothers, when you encounter various trials, for you know that the testing of your faith produces perseverance" —James 1: 2-3.

"A servant of God ought always to be happy" —St. Philip Neri.

"There is no joy like that known by the truly poor in spirit" —St. Therese of Lisieux.

"Joy is a net of love by which we catch souls" —St. Teresa of Calcutta.

"When large numbers of people share their joy in common, the happiness of each is greater because each adds fuel to the other's flame" —St. Augustine of Hippo.

"Joy, with peace, is the sister of charity. Serve the Lord with laughter" —St. Pio of Pietrelcina.

"You ask me whether or not I am in good spirits. How could I not be so? As long as Faith gives me strength, I will always be joyful" —St. Pier Giorgio Frassati.

"If we truly understand the Mass, we would die of joy" —St. Jean Marie Vianney.

Avalanche of Grace!

Day 44 – Prayer for the Virtue of Joy

Read God's Word: Isaiah 35: 1-10

O Father, who delights in the return of sinners!
O Jesus, Pure Joy, who lifts us from our misery!
O Holy Spirit, who helps us serve with laughter!

O Holy Trinity, may the *true joy* of living in You show:
in the trials, regrets, and sorrows I may carry;
in my comportment, words, gestures, and actions;
in the service of charity to kith and kin, and alien;
in favors received and not received in prayers;
in the mission that I am called to serve You;
and, in every type of suffering You have in store for me.

O Jesus, Sovereign Joy, let joy reign in my body!
O Jesus, Sovereign Joy, let joy reign in my soul!
O Jesus, Sovereign Joy, let joy reign in my spirit!

O Father, Absolute Joy, I yearn for everlasting joy!
O Jesus, Pure Joy, I yearn for final union with You!
O Holy Spirit, Simple Joy, may joy flow in me now!

Day 44 – A Story of Virtuous Joy

Kayla caught a co-worker in a lie and gently brought it to her attention. However, the co-worker claimed that the lie had nothing to do with her responsibilities as a waitress.

The co-worker complained to their supervisor about Kayla creating a hostile environment. Kayla asked, "When did friendly advice on telling the truth become the problem?"

The next day, Kayla pondered at Mass, "I forgive, I forgive."

Heaven rejoiced at that very moment as the priest's *Little Saint* escaped from his caretaker and ran down the aisle, skidding umpteen times, anxious to assist his master at the altar. Arriving just before the words of consecration, *Little Saint* doggishly scratched himself. Then, beside his master, he knelt and worshipped the Savior, as his master, *in persona Christi*, said, "Take this all of you and eat it, for this is My Body, which will be given up for you…"

Overflowing joy filled Kayla's heart – *even God's littlest of creatures knew His Real Presence.* Kayla bowed in adoration as Jesus healed her soul.

Jesus: *"My child, rejoice in the truth, for I am Truth."*

I: *"Jesus, You suffered lies, so I may live in joy forever."*

Avalanche of Grace!

Day 45 – Virtue of Interior Silence

Silence isn't something most people are used to and may even avoid. Many of us know the feeling of "awkward silence" or may have uttered the words "The silence is deafening" and yet the practice of silence is invaluable to aiding the spiritual life. It aids in keeping one from committing *sins of the tongue* and opening one to contemplation of God. However, silence is not an end in itself.

St. Abba Pimen said it perfectly: "A man may seem to be silent, but if his heart is condemning others, he is babbling ceaselessly. But there may be another who talks from morning till night and yet he is truly silent, that is, he says nothing that is not profitable."

Interior silence is the main goal of outer silence. Interior silence fosters prayer and enables one to hear God. It is the means to a deeper relationship with God—that which a Christian should be constantly striving after. A simple way to think of interior silence is to think of a close relationship you have with someone. In this relationship, when everything is good there is no awkward silence. Much is understood without being said; love is shared through a glance or gentle touch. Words are not needed. You and the other have a communion together; you see each other clearly and simply rest in one another's presence. Interior silence should lead us to this kind of relationship with God; we simply rest in His presence. ...

I have learned to love quiet but I am also an over thinker. Sometimes I like the quiet because it enables me to think. I have learned that this is not inner silence and will not lead to prayer. Once in confession when explaining some overwhelming thoughts I was having, the priest told me to take time to listen to my favorite kind of music for five to ten minutes each day as an antidote for the constant negative thinking. This was not the kind of advice I expected but I realized why he was telling me this. For some, physical silence may be unnerving, for people like myself, inner silence is hard to learn. Thinking about God even, is not the same as praying. Just like thinking of your spouse—even good, loving thoughts, is not the same as engaging in a relationship with your spouse. We can be thinking of someone and ignoring them at the same time. This is very easy to do with God. Learning inner silence, a silencing of thoughts and distractions, will help to lead us to real prayer. Again, balance is necessary. Silence for the sake of silence is not what we are after. A quieting of our lives, minds, and hearts should aid us to a deeper relationship with God. ...

We do not need to learn elaborate forms of prayer. We need to honestly, humbly, and lovingly approach God with a desire for communion with Him and He will respond. Focusing our inner attention on Him is something we can all learn to do. Our relationship with God isn't just for Sundays or formal prayer times.

Like the disciples on the road to Emmaus, we need our eyes to be opened to see that it is Christ our Lord who is always walking with us. The two disciples were too busy talking to each other about what happened to Jesus and too upset about what the meaning could be behind the women finding His tomb empty that they failed to recognize Jesus while He walked and talked with them (Luke 24:13-35). We can reasonably make an effort to lessen the noise in our lives which can help us to have inner silence so we don't also fail to see Jesus walking with us daily—in our own hearts, and the hearts of those around us.

(Excerpts from Jessica Archuleta's "Lessons from a Monastery.")

Day 45 – Reflections on the Virtue of Interior Silence

"When he broke open the seventh seal, there was silence in heaven – for about half an hour. And I saw that the seven angels who stood before God were given seven trumpets"
—Revelation 8: 1-2.

"The lover of silence draws close to God. He talks to Him in secret, and God enlightens him. Jesus, by His silence, shamed Pilate; and a man by his silence conquers vainglory"
—St. John Climacus.

"Silence does good to the soul" —St. Therese of Lisieux.

"The most generous choices, especially the persevering, are the fruit of profound and prolonged union with God in prayerful silence" —St. John Paul II.

"It is great wisdom to know how to be silent and to look at neither the remarks, nor the deeds, nor the lives of others"
—St. John of the Cross.

"In some causes, silence is dangerous" —St. Ambrose.

"Silence is God's first language" —St. John of the Cross.

"God speaks in the silence of the heart. Listening is the beginning of prayer" —St. Teresa of Calcutta.

Avalanche of Grace!

Day 45 – Prayer for the Virtue of Interior Silence

Read God's Word: Matthew 2

O Father, all creation grows in silence for final joy!
O Jesus, all angels cried silently at the cross!
O Holy Spirit, all human virtues You tenderly aid!

O Holy Trinity, strip me of *unholy silence* when:
I entertain thoughts that offend God and neighbor;
I imagine a life that is convenient and fruitless;
I play back memories that I previously left at the cross;
I do not defend my faith;
and, I do not defend human life in all its stages.

O Jesus, fill me with *holy silence* when:
I behold Your face in the Blessed Sacrament;
I ponder on Your Word and Your Holy Sacrifice;
I receive Communion, as I await our final union;
and, I act in Your Will, reflecting on my own end.

O Father, in silence, I desire to attain joy with You!
O Jesus, in silence, I desire mercy in obeying You!
O Holy Spirit, in silence, I desire Your gift of self!

Day 45 – A Story of Virtuous Interior Silence

Sister Josefa revealed the truth and fruit of silence to those who sought her counsel. She offered these pearls of wisdom:

"Interior silence envelopes a crying baby's heart and stills it when a mom's mere touch says, 'I am here. I love you. I will not leave you. You are safe.'"

"Unborn babies who were silenced despite their right to life, do grow up in heaven. They have child-like conversations in heaven like why geese honk or why *Goose Down* is a lovable fairy tale character. They forgive their grieving moms."

"In silence, *manga*'s buds, flowers, and fruit come to be – in that order, for silence is gracefully ordered and perpetuates order within a soul that buds, blooms, and bears fruit. The bud illumines the flower within, the flower displays its virtue, and the *manga* fruit delights the family that eats it."

Indeed, God touches the soul in silence and lets it grow, here or there, in perfect or not-so-perfect solitude, over conversations and meals that bring to life God in people and people in God.

Jesus: "My child, You grow in Me when you are silent."

I: "Jesus, I cherish my communions of silence in You."

Avalanche of Grace!

Day 46 – Virtue of Contemplation

[*The first secret of entering into communication with God is to find Him*]…So, the contemplative life has God as its object; the active life concerns itself with our neighbor. When the active life is the overflowing of the contemplative life, it is called the apostolic life. And this is the most perfect, since it supposes the plenitude of contemplation and the perfection of activity; it is, as it were, a synthesis of the active life and the contemplative life…

> *You must know how to find God*
> *and how to communicate with Him.*

In one manner or another, therefore, every interior life must in its final phase be the contemplative life. Well, then, to contemplate God, the first requisite is to encounter Him. And once we have encountered Him, we need to know the means whereby to enter into communication with Him.

All this seems to be the most simple and obvious thing in the world. For where is God? We do not have to ascend to Heaven to find Him. God is within us: "In Him we live, and move, and are." The divine Goodness has wished to remain with us, in our heart and in the tabernacle. Yet despite bearing God in our heart, and living in a divine atmosphere, and having Him in the tabernacle, how difficult it ever is to find God! Is not this "not finding" God the great torment of souls?...

If all people—the wise, the ignorant, the simple, the imperfect, and even the sinners—have the right to enter into communication with God, why is it difficult to do so in practice? The answer lies in this frequent complaint of pious souls: "I cannot pray." "How so, if prayer is, as it were, the breath of the soul?" "That is true. I feel the need to pray; I wish to do so; but I am not able. I cannot form a single act. I am dumb, deaf, dry; I cannot hear, or speak, or feel."

How can one explain these apparent contradictions? God stands near, yet we do not find Him. We can enter into communication with Him in all manner of ways, yet we do not succeed in doing so.

Here we meet with the key of the interior life. The explanation of these apparent contradictions lies in this: that our God is a hidden God, as the sacred Scriptures tell us. "Verily Thou art a hidden God." And a hidden God must be sought. If there is a secret hiding place in a room, and if there is a person concealed in it, we do not encounter him, even though he is near us. We do not even suspect his presence. Thus it is with God. He is a hidden God. He is present everywhere, but everywhere He is concealed: in the stars of the heavens, in the earth that supports us, in the air that we breathe, in the neighbors that surround us. But will we always discover God?

Consequently one of the secrets of the interior life consists, not in knowing where God is, because we already know that He is everywhere, but in knowing that, wherever He is, He is hidden. Hence, the secret of entering into communication with Him is to find Him.

The second secret is this: Once we have found God, how do we communicate with Him? Sacred Scripture tells us: "For my thoughts are not your thoughts: nor your ways my ways, saith the Lord." Herein is the source of our difficulty in communicating with Him,... He has His manner of approaching us, and we do not understand, for in reality, we wish that He would communicate with us in our way. For example, we believe that as often as God communicates with us, we must feel it, since we cannot imagine that communication with a beloved person, as our Lord is, could be dry and barren. But since the ways of God are different from ours, ninety-nine percent of the times that our Lord comes to us, we do not feel it. And this deludes us, and we believe we cannot communicate with our Lord because we cannot perceive Him.

To us, it seems that our Lord can have only a delicious sweetness... And sometimes it is thus. The coming of our Lord fills our hearts with sweetness. But God does not always taste the same. He is like the manna; He holds within Himself all savors.

St. Bernardine of Siena says that God has two savors: the savor of sweetness and the savor of bitterness.

When we feel our heart heavy, it is also God who draws near; it is Jesus who communicates with us — no matter how poorly we understand that He also possesses the savor of bitterness. Well does St. Thomas say that all our errors in the spiritual life flow from this: that we wish to measure divine things with our human criterion, which is so puny and paltry. How often, when we think that we are most distant from God, we are most closely united to Him!

According to my view, the secret and key of the interior life is this: Jesus is a hidden God; we must therefore seek Him. But in seeking Him, we must remember that the ways of God are very different from our ways. To know those ways and to seek God through them are the sole means of finding God and of uniting ourselves to Him.

(Excerpt from "Two Secrets to Becoming Contemplative" taken from an adapted chapter of Archbishop Luis M. Martinez's *Worshipping a Hidden God: Unlocking the Secrets of an Interior Life*.)

Day 46 – Reflections on the Virtue of Contemplation

"Be still and know that I am God" — Psalm 46:10.

"Seek by reading and you will find by meditating. Knock by praying and it will be opened to you in contemplation" — St. John of the Cross.

"Look, look on Jesus, poor and crucified. Look on this Holy One, who for your love has died, and remember as you contemplate the sacred mysteries, this Jesus whom you gaze upon, loves you most tenderly" — St. Clare of Assisi.

"Souls who aspire to a sublime union with God by contemplation usually suffer interior purgations in one way or another" — St. Paul of the Cross.

"I am mute and lost in God" — St. Catherine of Genoa.

"He who carries God in his heart bears heaven wherever He goes" — St. Ignatius of Loyola.

"Do not rush one prayer after another but say them with orderly deliberation as one addressing a great person for a favor. Do not just pay attention to the words, but rather let the mind be in the heart, standing before the Lord in full awareness of His Presence, in full consciousness of His greatness, and grace and justice" — St. Theophan the Recluse.

Avalanche of Grace!

Day 46 – *Prayer for the Virtue of Contemplation*

Read God's Word: John 20:1-18

O Father, whose gaze reveals that I am loved!
O Jesus, whose gaze reveals that I am valued!
O Holy Spirit, whose gaze reveals that I am to love!

Father, You gaze out my separation so I may be in You.
I fix my gaze upon Your Heart, Father, to love You.
Jesus, You gaze out my brokenness so I may be whole.
I fix my gaze on Your Sacred Heart to be healed.
Holy Spirit, You gaze out noise in me so I may be still.
I fix my gaze on Your Heart for You to work in mine.

Father, Your love hounds me. I am found by You.
Jesus, Your love purgates me. I live in and for You.
Holy Spirit, Your love impels me. I need You more.

O Father, in Your Heart's gaze, still me to love!
O Jesus, in Your Heart's gaze, still me to sacrifice!
O Holy Spirit, in Your Heart's gaze, still me to act!

Day 46 – A Story of Virtuous Contemplation

The priest's homily was simple, on the theme of, "Be still and know that I am God" (Psalm 46:10). Soon-to-be novice Betsy discerned God's will by reflecting on this same scripture verse in the depths of her heart. She shared this with Tricia, the youth coordinator of her Basic Ecclesial Community (BEC).

A day later, during a home visit, the head of the household shared with Tricia, "In all my suffering, I know my Lord and my God says, 'Be still and know that I am God'." There arose a desire in Tricia's heart to be still, to *know* God as others did. How do *they* get to know God? Why is God so real in their lives?

Tricia's first inner locution happened in the middle of the night while she was asleep. The Holy Spirit prompted her to sit up and she heard His voice in the depths of her soul, "Be still and know that I am God." *The same words as were given to other souls.*

Tricia felt the warmth of His love overcome her spirit and soul. In stillness, she *knew* God, who *knew her* from the time she was conceived. A desire for perfect union with God took root in Tricia's soul as she broke away many times during the day to be with God.

Jesus: "My child, desire Me. I am the Word made flesh."

I: "Jesus, I fix my eyes on You. Enflesh me in You."

Avalanche of Grace!

Day 47 – Virtue of Gratitude

Let us attempt to obtain a view of this gradually disappearing virtue – gratitude. Let us ask what is necessary so that gratitude may become possible.

Above all there is this: We can be grateful only to a person. Gratitude and petition are possible only between an "I" and a "Thou." We cannot thank a law, a board, or a company. We may do so out of mere politeness when the proper sum is handed to us, in order to keep everything in the domain of good manners, but real gratitude does not enter into the matter, for gratitude is the expression of a personal encounter in human need.

But two persons, one of whom is situated so that he has something or can do something, while the other has not or cannot – these stand face to face. The one asks and the other is ready; the one gives and the other thanks; and the two are united by a human tie. Here gratitude is possible and it becomes a basis for community.

Furthermore, gratitude is possible only in the realm of freedom. For the fact that the sun rises in the morning or, to express it scientifically, that the earth comes into such a position in relation to the sun that it becomes visible: for this I am not grateful. It is certainly true that on a bright morning very lively sentiments of gratitude may arise because something so powerful and beautiful is taking place. But these are the responses of man to Him who has created all, or else they are the after effects of a time in which the sun itself was revered as a divinity. ...

(Excerpt from Fr. Romano Guardini's "The Virtue of Gratitude.")

Avalanche of Grace!

Day 47 – Reflections on the Virtue of Gratitude

"Give thanks to the LORD, for he is good, His mercy endures forever" —Psalm 118:1.

"The secret to happiness is to live moment by moment and to thank God for what He is sending us every day in His goodness" —St. Gianna Berreta Molla.

"Remember the past with gratitude, live the present with enthusiasm, look forward to the future with confidence" — St. John Paul II.

"He who loves with purity considers not the gift of the lover but the love of the giver" —Thomas a Kempis.

"I would maintain that gratitude is the highest form of thought, and that gratitude is happiness doubled by wonder" —G.K. Chesterton.

"Jesus does not demand great actions from us, but simply surrender and gratitude" —St. Therese of Lisieux.

"No duty is more urgent than that of returning thanks" —St. Ambrose of Milan.

"Gratitude is the first sign of a thinking, rational creature" —Blessed Solanus Casey.

Avalanche of Grace!

Day 47 – Prayer for the Virtue of Gratitude

Read God's Word: Luke 17:11-19

O Father, thank You for the holy gift of life!
O Jesus, You are the greatest gift given to me!
O Holy Spirit, Love of the Giver of all Grace!

I thank You for the thought You had of me!
I thank You that I am wonderfully made!
I thank You for breathing Your *ruach** into my soul!
I thank You for my childhood, youth, and old age!
I thank You for my family and community!
I thank You for every sunrise and sunset!
Stir my heart and soul to thank you in trying times.
I offer up all my wounds in union with Yours!
I offer up all my sufferings in union with Yours!
I offer up all my loneliness in union with Yours!

O Father, I thank You for You are my Father!
O Jesus, I thank You – my source and summit!
O Holy Spirit, I thank You for always loving me!

*ruach – Hebrew – "breath,""wind," or "spirit."

Day 47 – A Story of Virtuous Gratitude

Elizabeth thought the worst. She had done her part in getting ready for her economics final exam. Here she was, in the most beautiful college in the US, with a sweet dream of achieving an accounting degree in two years. She had even volunteered her time with the less advantaged to help them prepare their taxes that spring.

Surely, God knew her heart. *How do I tell my parents that I am failing economics? How do I tell them that I might spiral down to becoming a college drop-out? How do I face myself and the world?* In tears, she faced her fears and told her mom. In response, Mom texted her Psalm 47 and comforted her.

Mom and her prayer partners went into praise and thanksgiving mode for victory. They prayed that God would do exceedingly well for both Elizabeth and her friends who had taken the same exam. God came through, with Elizabeth placing at the top of the class and all her classmates passing the course!

Jesus: "My Child, Your beatitude of gratitude allows for more latitude of My Mercy to be poured out."

I: "Jesus, I want to thank You in all of the unknowns."

Avalanche of Grace!

Day 48 – Virtue of Praise

Praise is the form of prayer which recognizes most immediately that God is God. It lauds God for His own sake and gives Him glory, quite beyond what he does, but simply because HE IS. It shares in the blessed happiness of the pure of heart who love God in faith before seeing him in glory. By praise, the Spirit is joined to our spirits to bear witness that we are children of God, testifying to the only Son in whom we are adopted and by whom we glorify the Father. Praise embraces the other forms of prayer and carries them toward Him who is its source and goal: the "one God, the Father, from whom are all things and for whom we exist."

Prayer of praise is entirely disinterested and rises to God, lauds Him, and gives Him glory for His own sake, quite beyond what He has done, but simply because HE IS.

(Catechism of the Catholic Church, 2639, 2649)

Avalanche of Grace!

Day 48 – Reflections on the Virtue of Praise

"Hallelujah!
Praise God in his holy sanctuary;
give praise in the mighty dome of heaven.
Give praise for his mighty deeds,
praise him for his great majesty.
Give praise with blasts upon the horn,
praise him with harp and lyre.
Give praise with tambourines and dance,
praise him with strings and pipes.
Give praise with crashing cymbals,
praise him with sounding cymbals.
Let everything that has breath
give praise to the LORD!
Hallelujah!" (Psalm 150:1-6)

"It is not enough that I should praise God by myself: I must help the hearts of all to love Him and the tongues of all to praise Him" —St. Ignatius of Loyola.

"The earth is filled with tabernacles, praise Him" —St. Luigi Guanella.

"The truly humble reject all praise for themselves, and refer it all to God" —St. Francis de Sales.

Avalanche of Grace!

Day 48 – Prayer for the Virtue of Praise

Read God's Word: Daniel 3: 1-100

Blessed be God! Blessed be Your Holy Name!
Blessed be Jesus Christ, true God and true Man!
Blessed be the Holy Spirit, the Paraclete!

All creation and creatures praise You, God!
Praise Your Holy Name! You are the Lord!
Praise Your Holy Cross! You are Savior!
Praise Your Holy Temple! You died for all!
Praise Your Sacred Body! You are Healer!
Praise Your Precious Blood! You are Deliverer!
Praise Your Pierced Heart! You love all infinitely!
Praise Your Holy Sacrifice! You are in me, Lord!
Praise Your Holy Trinity! I am totally yours, Lord!
Praise Your Holy Wounds! You are Mercy!

O Father, You are Uncreated and Unchanging!
O Jesus, You are Truly Present in the Eucharist!
O Holy Spirit, change me to praise Jesus always!

Day 48 – A Story of Virtuous Praise

MacKenzie and Joe's son Noah, 13, was diagnosed with bleeding in the brain. A lack of oxygen and nutrients caused tissues to gradually die, and infection had set into dead cells. He could not take any medication because of the risk of blood clots. The prognosis – amputate both legs. But, pre-surgery tests ruled out the procedure as his condition was so bad that it would be a death sentence for the young teen.

In their quiet desperation, Mackenzie and Joe turned completely to God, begging Him to show His Mercy on Noah. Prayer warrior friends stormed heaven with their praises, "Jesus, You are the Healer! You are faithful and true! You, almighty God, can heal NOW – not then, not in two months, and not in a year but NOW." Jesus healed Noah, and his legs began to improve day by day. Within weeks, Noah had a clean bill of health.

At times, doctors cancel a surgery as they cannot heal. At times, God cancels a surgery because He does heal – He is the Healer. God moves in when we look up to Him, hands raised like a child.

Jesus: *"My Child, I love your praises! I can heal you."*

I: *"Jesus, I praise and thank You for healing me. Please heal all who need healing right now, and by Your Will."*

Avalanche of Grace!

Day 49 – Virtue of Awe

Imagine eating the sun—and imagine you could do it without perishing. What would happen? You would receive into your body the source of light and warmth. You would have within you all the light and heat that you could possibly ever need or want. No more heating bills, no more light-bulbs, no more winter trips to warmer climes.

When we receive Jesus in the Most Blessed Sacrament, we receive the source of all supernatural light and warmth, the light of truth, the heat of love, for indeed He is the "sun of Justice." We receive God Himself, the very Son of God, Who is inseparable from the Father and the Holy Spirit. Saint Ephrem […]wrote:

> He called the bread his living body and he filled it with himself and his Spirit ... He who eats it with faith, eats Fire and Spirit ... Take and eat this, all of you, and eat with it the Holy Spirit. For it is truly my body and whoever eats it will have eternal life. (1)

That we are not killed instantly by this contact with eternal and infinite Fire is, in its own way, a greater miracle than would be eating the sun without perishing. Our Lord protects us, courteously hiding His blazing glory lest we be overwhelmed, and gently radiating His peace. …

(Excerpt from Dr. Peter Kwasniewski's "Eating Fire and Spirit: The Most Wondrous of All God's Gifts.")

Avalanche of Grace!

Day 49 – Reflections on the Virtue of Awe

"Fire and heat, bless the Lord; praise and exalt him above all forever. Cold and chill, bless the Lord; praise and exalt him above all forever. Dew and rain, bless the Lord; praise and exalt him above all forever" — Daniel 3: 66-68.

"It would be easier for the earth to exist without the sun than without the sacrifice of the Holy Mass" — St. Pio of Pietrelcina.

"In my deepest wound, I saw Your glory and it dazzled me" — St. Augustine of Hippo.

"The highest form of prayer is to stand in awe of God" — St. Isaac the Syrian.

"The beauty of being alive is that we can always start all over again" — St. Bernadette Soubirous.

"The world will never lack for wonders. Only for a lack of wonder" — G.K. Chesterton.

"He is not past, He is present now. And though He is not seen, He is here now. The same God who walked the water, who did miracles, etc, is in the Tabernacle. We come before Him, we speak to Him just as He was spoken to…years ago" — St. John Henry Newman.

Avalanche of Grace!

Day 49 – Prayer for the Virtue of Awe

Read God's Word: Psalm 145: 1-21

O Father, God of all resplendence and simplicity!
O Jesus, Real Presence — a wonder then and now!
O Holy Spirit, Advocate for savoring His wonders!

Open my eyes, ears, and heart to dwell upon how:
awesome You are, God of the universe!
awesome You are in sending Jesus to die for me;
awesome You are to become Body and Blood;
awesome You are to wait for me in the tabernacle;
awesome You are to invite me to sup with You;
awesome You are to show Your glory in my hurts;
awesome You are to let me start again, *nunc coepi;*
awesome You are in inhabiting my spirit; and,
and, awesome You are in staying with me eternally!

O Father, I am littlest in Your sublime creation!
O Jesus, Your tininess in the host makes us a pair!
O Holy Spirit, Your breath inspires me to linger!

*nunc coepi – Latin, "Now, I begin."

Day 49 – A Story of Virtuous Awe

Lucy had trust issues due to failed relationships. No one could feel or see her hurt. There she was as usual at the weekly Healing Mass in Waltham, MA. During a healing prayer before the Blessed Sacrament, she went down in the spirit as the priest, who has a special charism for healing, laid his hands on her forehead.

Then, the Holy Spirit stirred her spirit and she experienced tremendous joy and began laughing; it started softly and then got stronger. It was a sweet laughter that filled the air like the incense from the thurifier. "Holy Spirit, please stop," she said joyfully.

Lucy, then, saw in a vision that she was in the water like Peter about to drown but did not. Why? The Holy Spirit was causing her to roll in laughter. As she could not swim, fear arose in her heart. "Lord, save me," she said, reflecting Peter's words.

As the vision continued, she saw Jesus' mother come close to her; Lucy could only see Mary's mantle and so grabbed on to its hem. The *winds* dropped; Lucy sailed to harbor in Mary.

Jesus: "My Beloved, My Presence heals. For where I am, the Holy Spirit is. And, He dwells in My Mother, too."

I: "Jesus, Your Presence heals all my wounds."

Day 50 – Virtue of Adoration

God makes himself known by recalling his all-powerful loving, and liberating action in the history of the one he addresses: "I brought you out of the land of Egypt, out of the house of bondage." The first word contains the first commandment of the Law: "You shall fear the LORD your God; you shall serve him. . . . You shall not go after other gods."[5] God's first call and just demand is that man accept him and worship him.

Adoration is the first act of the virtue of religion. To adore God is to acknowledge him as God, as the Creator and Savior, the Lord and Master of everything that exists, as infinite and merciful Love. "You shall worship the Lord your God, and him only shall you serve," says Jesus, citing *Deuteronomy*.[13]

To adore God is to acknowledge, in respect and absolute submission, the "nothingness of the creature" who would not exist but for God. To adore God is to praise and exalt him and to humble oneself, as Mary did in the *Magnificat*, confessing with gratitude that he has done great things and holy is his name.[14] The worship of the one God sets man free from turning in on himself, from the slavery of sin and the idolatry of the world.

(Catechism of the Catholic Church 2084, 2096-2097)

Avalanche of Grace!

Day 50 – Reflections on the Virtue of Adoration

"Thomas answered and said to him, 'My Lord and my God!'"
—John 20:28.

"If we get in front of the sun, we get a sun tan, but if we get in front of Jesus in the Eucharist, we become saints"
—Carlos Acutis, Servant of God.

"I adore You, Lord and Creator, hidden in the Most Blessed Sacrament"—St. Faustina Kowalska.

"God is as really present in the Holy Eucharist as He is in the glory of heaven"—St. Paschal Baylon.

"The greatest story of all time is contained in a white host"
—Blessed Fulton Sheen.

"There are two things the devil is deadly afraid of: fervent communions and frequent visits to the Blessed Sacrament"
—St. John Bosco.

"Receive communion often and Jesus will change you into Himself"—St. Peter Julian Eymard.

"The soul as soon as it comes to know Me [God], reaches out to love her neighbors"—St. Catherine of Siena.

Avalanche of Grace!

Day 50 – Prayer for the Virtue of Adoration

Read God's Word: Luke 7: 36-50

O Father, I love and adore Your Heart!
O Jesus, I love and adore Your Heart!
O Holy Spirit, I love and adore Your Heart!

Holy Trinity –
I adore You for You alone love each other purely!
I adore You for You alone are lovely, my first lover!
I adore You for You alone are my Savior!;
I adore You for You alone are holy and worthy!
I adore You for You alone are loving and forgiving!
I adore You for You alone are the sweetest fragrance!
I adore You for You alone can feed my soul!
I adore You for You alone heal my wounds!
I adore You for You alone are my greatest longing!

O Father, I desire You as You desire me!
O Jesus, I want to wash Your feet with my tears!
O Holy Spirit, I delight in You as You in me!

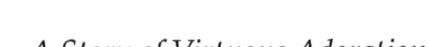

Day 50 – A Story of Virtuous Adoration

"The sun and bright lights bother me," Tom complained. It started when he believed the optometrist's report that there were cataract deposits in his eyes and that it comes with age. Fear set in — Tom was twelve years from retirement. "Me? Old?"

In his desperation, an inner voice asked him: "Will you love, adore, and trust in Me, in the Blessed Sacrament? I am Eternal." Tom thought with a moment of guilt – adoration had taken a back-seat. He also went to the Sacrament of Reconciliation and confessed his sins.

With new vigor Tom said, "Jesus, You are the Son of Man and God, who is bigger and more radiant than the sun! Jesus, I am going to fix my eyes on You in the Blessed Sacrament until You heal me, only if You will it." So Tom renewed his commitment to God to adore Him.

After the second week of doing a holy hour, Tom knew that his eyes were back to normal. The sun and lights no longer bothered him. Jesus healed his eyes as Tom spent time gazing upon Him.

Jesus: "My Little One, I gaze into your heart, soul, and spirit when you adore Me."

I: "I love You, Jesus! I want to gaze upon You forever."

References and Notes

All sources have been used with permission.

Day 1 *Faith*
Catechism of the Catholic Church (CCC). Excerpts from the English translation of the *Catechism of the Catholic Church* for use in the United States of America Copyright © 1994, United States Catholic Conference, Inc. —Libreria Editrice Vaticana. Used with Permission. English translation of the *Catechism of the Catholic Church*: Modifications from the Editio Typica copyright © 1997, United States Conference of Catholic Bishops—Libreria Editrice Vaticana

CCC. Ibid. ¶1812- ¶1816
78 *DV* 5.
79 *Rom* 1:17; *Gal* 5:6.
80 Cf. Council of Trent (1547): DS 1545.
81 *Jas* 2:26.
82 *LG* 42; cf. *DH* 14.
83 *Mt* 10:32-33.

Day 2 *Hope*
CCC. Ibid. ¶1817-¶1821
84 *Heb* 10:23.
85 *Titus* 3:6-7.
86 Cf. *Gen* 17:4-8; 22:1-18.
87 *Rom* 4:18.
88 *Rom* 5:5.
89 *Heb* 6:19-20.
90 *1 Thess* 5:8.
91 *Rom* 12:12.
92 Cf. *Rom* 8:28-30; *Mt* 7:21.
93 *Mt* 10:22; cf. Council of Trent: DS 1541.
94 *1 Tim* 2:4.
95 St. Teresa of Avila, *Excl.* 15:3.

Day 3 *Charity*
CCC. Ibid. ¶1822-1829
96 Cf. *Jn* 13:34.
97 *Jn* 13:1.
98 *Jn* 15:9,12.
99 *Jn* 15:9-10; cf. *Mt* 22:40; *Rom* 13:8-10.
100 *Rom* 5:10.
101 Cf. *Mt* 5:44; *Lk* 10:27-37; *Mk* 9:37; *Mt* 25:40, 45.
102 *1 Cor* 13:4-7.
103 *1 Cor* 13:1-4.
104 *1 Cor* 13:13.
105 *Col* 3:14.
106 Cf. *1 Jn* 4:19.
107 St. Basil, Reg. fus. tract., prol. 3 PG 31, 896 B.
108 St. Augustine, In ep. Jo. 10, 4: PL 35, 2057.

Day 4 *Prudence*
CCC. Ibid. ¶1833-¶1835
YOUCAT. 173 (English).
Cardinal Christoph
Schoenborn. Translated
by Michael. J. Miller. San
Francisco, CA: Ignatius Press,
2011. www.ignatius.com

Day 5 *Justice*
CCC. Ibid. ¶1836
YOUCAT. Ibid. 173-174.

Day 6 *Fortitude*
CCC. Ibid. ¶1809, ¶1837
YOUCAT. Ibid. 174.

Day 7 *Temperance*
CCC. Ibid. ¶1809, ¶1838
YOUCAT. Ibid. 174.

Day 8 *Poverty*
CCC. Ibid. ¶ 2446
239 AA 8 # 5.
240 St. Gregory the Great,
Regula Pastoralis. 3, 21:
PL 77, 87.
241 Cf. ⇨ Isa 58:6-7;
⇨ Heb 13:3.
YOUCAT. Ibid. 174.

Day 9 *Mourning*
CCC. Ibid. ¶ 2300, 1032
92 Cf. Tob 1:16-18
609 2 Macc 12:46.
610 Cf. Council of Lyons II
(1274):DS 856.

611 St. John Chrysostom,
Hom. in 1 Cor. 41,5:PG 61,361;
cf. *Job* 1:5.

Day 10 *Meekness*
De Marco, Dr. Donald. "Virtue
of Meekness." *Lay Witness*
(May 1999). Reprinted in
Catholic Education Resource
Center (CERC)
www.catholiceducation.org/en/
culture/catholic-contributions/
the-virtue-of-meekness.html
De Sales, St. Francis.
Introduction to the Devout Life.
Tr. and Ed. John K. Ryan. New
York: Image Books Doubleday.
1989. Print.

Day 11 *Righteousness*
Kreeft, Dr. Peter. "Happiness:
Blessed Are Those Who
Hunger and Thirst for
Righteousness" from "Part 3:
Blessed are Those Who Hunger
and Thirst for Righteousness,"
a talk given by Dr. Peter Kreeft
in various places at various
times. 2012.
Ibid. CERC www.
catholiceducation.org/en/
religion-and-philosophy/
philosophy/happiness-blessed-
are-those-who-hunger-and-
thirst-for-righteousness.html

Day 12 *Mercy*
Sri, Dr. Edward. "Understanding Relativism with Mercy." *Who am I to Judge? Responding to Relativism with Logic and Love* San Francisco: Ignatius Press, Greenwood Village: Augustine Institute, 2016. www.ignatius.com

Day 13 *Cleanliness of Heart*
CCC. Ibid. ¶2517-¶2520
305 *Mt* 15:19.
306 *Pastor Hermae*, Mandate 2,1:PG 2,916.
307 *Mt* 5:8.
308 Cf. *1 Tim* 4:3-9; *2 Tim* 2:22.
309 Cf. *1 Thess* 4:7; *Col* 3:5; *Eph* 4:19.
310 Cf. *Titus* 1:15; *1 Tim* 1:3-4; *2 Tim* 2:23-26.
311 St. Augustine, *Defide et symbolo* 10,25:PL 40,196.
312 Cf. *1 Cor* 13:12; *1 Jn* 3:2.

Day 14 *Peace-Making*
Swetland, Msgr. Stuart. "A Primer on Peace." March 1, 2007. Catholic Answers. www.catholic.com/magazine/print-edition/a-primer-on-peace

Day 15 *Resilience*
Wicks, Dr. Robert J. *Bounce: Living the Resilient Life* as reprinted in Rick Heffern's "Make a Difference in the World by Being Resilient." Dec. 11, 2009. *National Catholic Register* www.ncronline.org/news/spirituality/make-difference-world-being-resilient

Day 16 *Contrition*
Maturin, Fr. Basil. *Spiritual Guidelines for Souls Seeking God* as reflected in "Nurture Genuine Sorrow for Your Sins." March 7, 2017. www.catholicexchange.com/contrition-nurture-genuine-sorrow-sins

Day 17 *Repentance*
Wilson, Alfred. CP. "Remorse and Repentance." Excerpts from *Pardon and Peace.* www.catholictradition.org/Christ/repentance.htm

Day 18 *Reparation*
CCC. Ibid. ¶2453-¶2454
CCC. Ibid. ¶2504-¶2510

Day 19 *Balanced Passions*
CCC. Ibid. ¶1762-¶1775
40 Cf. *Mk* 7:21.
41 St. Thomas Aquinas, *STh* I-II,26 4, *corp. art.*
42 Cf. St. Augustine, *De Trin.*, 8,3,4:PL 42,949-950.
43 St. Augustine, *De civ. Dei* 14,7,2:PL 41,410.

44 St. Thomas Aquinas, *STh* I-II,24,1 *corp. art.*
45 Cf. St. Thomas Aquinas, *STh* I-II,24,3.
46 *Ps* 84:2.

Day 20 *Moral Conscience*
CCC. Ibid. ¶1776-¶1788
47 *GS* 16.
48 Cf. *Rom* 2:14-16.
49 Cf. *Rom* 1:32.
50 John Henry Cardinal Newman, "Letter to the Duke of Norfolk," V, in *Certain Difficulties felt by Anglicans in Catholic Teaching* II (London: Longmans Green, 1885), 248.
51 St. Augustine, *In ep Jo.* 8,9:PL 35,2041.
52 *1 Jn* 3:19-20.
53 *DH* 3 § 2.
54 Cf. *Ps* 119:105.
55 Cf. *DH* 14.

Day 21 *Detachment*
Warren, Rev. Cornelius J. C. SS.R. Adapted from the German of Rev. Paul Leick's writings based on the works of St. Alphonsus Liguori's *The 12 Steps to Holiness and Salvation.* Rockford, IL: TAN, 1986.

Day 22 *Total Abandonment*
de Caussade, Rev. Jean-Pierre. S.J. *Abandonment to Divine Providence.* Translated. Ed. J Ramiere from the Complete Tenth Edition by E. J. Strickland. St. Louis: B. Heder Book Company, 1921. Grand Rapids, MI: Christian Classics Ethereal Library. www.ccel.org/d/decaussade/abandonment/cache/abandonment.pdf

Day 23 *Sacrifice*
Kowalska, St. Maria Faustina. *Diary: Divine Mercy in My Soul*, Notebook VI, #1767. 3rd Ed. Stockbridge, MA: Congregation of Marians, 2003. Used with permission of the Marian Fathers of the Immaculate Conception of the B.V.M.

Day 24 *Holy Indifference*
Broom OMV, Fr. Ed. "What the 2 Maccabees Can Teach Us about Holy Indifference?" Feb. 26, 2019. www.catholicexchange.com/what-2-maccabees-can-teach-us-about-holy-indifference

Day 25 *Solidarity*
CCC. Ibid. ¶1939-¶1942
45 Cf. John Paul II, *SRS* 38-40; *CA* 10.

46 Pius XII, *Summi pontificatus*, October 20, 1939; AAS 31 (1939) 423 ff.
47 *Mt* 6:33.
48 Pius XII, Discourse, June 1, 1941.

Day 26 *Kindness and Goodness*
Hooser, Don. "Kindness from the Heart to the Helping Hand." www.ucg.org/the-good-news/the-fruit-of-the-spirit-kindness-from-the-heart-to-the-helping-hand
— "Goodness: God's Character and Humanity's Potential." www.ucg.org/the-good-news/the-fruit-of-the-spirit-goodness-gods-character-and-mans-potential

Day 27 *Respect for Life*
Dolan, Cardinal Timothy. "Lack of Respect for Life Leads to Other Problems."
Oct. 24, 2018. www.cny.org/stories/lack-of-respect-for-life-leads-to-other-problems,18061
CCC. Ibid. ¶2318-¶2329

Day 28 *Industry And Diligence*
Escriva, St. Josemaria. "Working Conscientiously."
1. *The Forge*, 698
2. Cf. *The Way*, 359
3. *Friends of God*, 55
4. *Furrow*, 527

Day 29 *Hospitality*
Toups, Jay. "Catholic Hospitality" *Catholic, Catholic Social Doctrine, and Generosity.* www.thestormatimeofmercy/wordpress.com/2018/04/16/catholic-hospitality

Day 30 *Magnanimity*
Fullam, Lisa. "Humility and Magnanimity in Spiritual Guidance." *Reflective Practice: Formation and Supervision in Ministry.* Vol 32: 36-47. www.journals.sfu.ca/rpfs/index.php/rpfs/article/view/58/57. Creative Commons Attribution-NonCommercial 3.0 Unported License.
[6] Ibid. Fullam, Lisa. Thomas began the *Summa Theologiae* in about 1265 and died in 1274, leaving it unfinished.
In the text, it is possible to see development of his thought on various questions. For a more complete account of his work on humility, see my book *The Virtue of Humility: A Thomistic Apologetic* (New York: The Edwin Mellen Press, 2009).

Day 31 *Orderliness*
Newsome, Dc. Matthew. "The Order of Our Lives." June 27, 2019.
www.wcucatholic.org/the-order-of-our-lives/

Day 32 *Discernment*
Thibodeaux S.J., Mark Fr. Interviewed by Fr. Sean Salai S.J. "Discerning Good and Bad Spirits: Wisdom from a Jesuit Spiritual Writer." *America: The Jesuit Review*. Jan. 11, 2017. www.americamagazine.org/faith/2017/01/11/discerning-good-and-bad-spirits-wisdom-jesuit-spiritual-writer

Day 33
O'Mara, Annet. March 1, 2020.

Day 34 *Honor And Integrity*
DeMarco, Dr. Donald. "The Virtue of Integrity." *Lay Witness*. 1999.
www.catholiceducation.org/en/culture/catholic-contributions/the-virtue-of-integrity.html

Day 35 *Faithfulness*
Marcos, JJ. "Learning to be Faithful." *Opus Dei*. Aug. 22, 2014. www.opusdei.org/en-us/article/learning-to-be-faithful/

Day 36 *Accountability*
De La Torre, Dr. Marlon. *Is Holding Someone Accountable a Virtue?* March 13, 2018.
www.northtexascatholic.org/catechesis-column-article?r=MF105XKZAV

Day 37 *Docility*
"Virtue of Docility." Companions of the Cross.
www.companionscross.org/lay-formation/developing-evangelical-heart/docility
All Formation Courses by Companions of the Cross are licensed under a Creative Commons Attribution-NonCommercial 3.0 Unported License.

Day 38 *Simplicity*
Metts, Sarah. "The Simplicity of Saint Vincent de Paul." Sept. 27, 2017.
www.catholicexchange.com/simplicity-st-vincent-de-paul

Day 39 *Humility*
Thomas, John Paul. *The Path to Holiness: Becoming a Living Sacrifice of Love*.
www.mycatholic.life/books/the-path-to-holiness/ch-2-the-virtue-of-humility/

Day 40 *Trust*
Thomas, John Paul. *The Path to Holiness: Becoming a Living Sacrifice of Love.* www.mycatholic.life/books/the-path-to-holiness/ch-3-the-virtue-of-trust/

Day 41 *Forgetting the Past*
St. John of the Cross. *Ascent of Mount Carmel.* Contemporary English Version. Ed. Henry L. Carrigan Jr. Book III, Ch. 2, 5.-6., 111-112, and Ch. 3, 3.-5., 113-114). Paraclete Press, 2010. Licensee: Aquinas Press, 2017.

Day 42 *Beauty*
O'Mara, Annet. March 13, 2020.

Day 43 *Holiness*
CCC. Ibid. ¶2013-¶2014
45 Cf. John Paul II, SRS 38 40; CA 10.
46 Pius XII, Summi pontificatus, October 20, 1939; AAS 31 (1939) 423 ff.
47 ⇨ Mt 6:33.
48 Pius XII, Discourse, June 1, 1941.

Day 44 *Joy*
Hruska, Elizabeth. "The Difference between Joy and Happiness." Sept. 27, 2004.
www.catholicexchange.com/the-difference-between-joy-and-happiness.

Day 45 *Interior Silence*
Archuleta, Jessica. "Lessons from a Monastery." March 4, 2015. www.catholicexchange.com/lessons-monastery-silence

Day 46 *Contemplation*
Martinez. Archbishop Luis M. "Two Secrets to Becoming Contemplative" taken from an adapted chapter of Archbishop Luis M. Martinez's *Worshipping a Hidden God: Unlocking the Secrets of an Interior Life.* May 17, 2016. www.catholicexchange.com/two-secrets-to-becoming-contemplative

Day 47 *Gratitude*
Guardini, Fr. Romano. "The Virtue of Gratitude." Nov. 27, 2014.
© 2020 *The Catholic Thing*. www.thecatholicthing.org/2014/11/27/the-virtue-of-gratitude/

Day 48 *Holiness*
CCC. Ibid. ¶2639
121 Cf. *Rom* 8:16.
122 *1 Cor* 8:6.
CCC. Ibid. ¶2649

Day 49 *Awe*
Kwasniewski, Dr. Peter. "Eating Fire and Spirit: The Most Wondrous of All God's Gifts." May 30, 2018. www.onepeterfive.com/eating-fire-and-spirit-the-most-wondrous-of-all-gods-gifts/

[1] *Sermo IV in Hebdomadam Sanctam*: CSCO 413/Syr. 182, 55, quoted by St. John Paul II, Encyclical Letter *Ecclesia de Eucharistia* (April 17, 2003), n. 17.

Day 50 *Adoration*
CCC. Ibid. ¶2084
5 *Deut* 6:13-14.
CCC. Ibid. ¶2096-¶2097
13 *Lk* 4:8; Cf. *Deut* 6:13.
14 Cf. *Lk* 1:46-49.

Catholic saints' quotes. Retrieved from google.com
Multiple URL links.
Origins trace to print or oral tradition sources.

Lightning Source UK Ltd.
Milton Keynes UK
UKHW020631030920
369287UK00010B/281